SAM THE COOKING GUY: BETWEEN THE BUNS

SAM THE COOKING GUY:

BETWEEN THE BUNS

Burgers, Sandwiches, Tacos,
Burritos, Hot Dogs, and More

Countryman Press

An Imprint of W. W. Norton & Company
Independent Publishers Since 1923

SAM ZIEN

For information about permission to reproduce selections from this book, write to
Permissions, Countryman Press, 500 Fifth Avenue, New York, NY 10110

For information about special discounts for bulk purchases, please contact
W. W. Norton Special Sales at specialsales@wwnorton.com or 800-233-4830

Manufacturing by TC Transcontinental
Book design by Allison Chi
Production managers: Gwen Cullen and Devon Zahn

Library of Congress Cataloging-in-Publication Data

Names: Zien, Sam, author.
Title: Sam the Cooking Guy. Between the buns : burgers, sandwiches, tacos, burritos, hot dogs, and more / Sam Zien.
Description: New York, NY : Countryman Press, [2022] | Includes index.
Identifiers: LCCN 2021057200 | ISBN 9781682686881 | ISBN 9781682686898 (epub)
Subjects: LCSH: Sandwiches. | Stuffed foods (Cooking) | Quick and easy cooking. | LCGFT: Cookbooks.
Classification: LCC TX818 .Z54 2022 | DDC 641.84—dc23/eng/20211122
LC record available at https://lccn.loc.gov/2021057200

Countryman Press
www.countrymanpress.com

An imprint of W. W. Norton & Company, Inc.
500 Fifth Avenue, New York, NY 10110
www.wwnorton.com

10 9 8 7 6 5 4 3 2 1

Dedicated to you guys—this book is for all of you. The subscribers, the followers, the watchers, the buy-our-merchandisers, the come-into-the-restauranters, the "Hi-Sam"-as-you're-walking-down-the-streeters, the "I-couldn't-cook-but-now-I-can"ers—all of you.

You made this possible, so in a sense this is also your book. But don't get any ideas about me sharing any of my earnings with you. I appreciate you, but I'm not crazy.

THANK YOU

Beth—for keeping me organized.

Deb—for keeping this book organized.

Lucas—great working with you again—your pictures and work style are the best.

Michael—thanks for believing again.

Ann—I couldn't have asked for anyone better to have grabbed the baton.

Jessica, Rhina, Allison—you guys make this really easy.

Leigh—thank you for everything. By the way, more Bubble Wrap is coming, and you can't stop it.

My family—I'm so lucky. Oh . . . and hi, little Rio :)

The Shuneems—you two are always the best. No help, but the best.

Kelly—just know that none of this would be any fun or have been worth it at all without you.
Love you so so much.

CONTENTS

INTRODUCTION

WHAT MAKES IT a burger? The bun.

What makes it a sandwich? The bread.

What makes it a taco . . . okay, I think you get where this is going.

And it really makes no difference what goes between the buns, the slices of bread, or even between the tortillas—it's still a hamburger, a sandwich, a burrito, or a taco. This book is about all of those and their beautiful, crispy, cheesy, melty, toasty, warm deliciousness.

On some level—make that many levels—this is a book about comfort food, just not the macaroni and cheese kind. Well, actually, there is some of that. In any case, the stuff in this book is comforting to eat, but I think wouldn't generally be labeled as "comfort."

But that said, if you can't find something in this book to love, the book is not the problem. Because somewhere in this collection of recipes for burgers, sandwiches, tacos, burritos, and hot dogs, even the most finicky eater has to find something to love. It's like the food equivalent of showing someone a room full of puppies—because even the biggest asshole is gonna smile, bend down, and wanna pick one up.

And before there's any carb shaming, look what Harvard Medical School wrote:

"Carbohydrates are foods that get converted into glucose, which is a main source of fuel for our body. It is especially important for the brain."

Or *US News & World Report*:

"Eating carbohydrates boosts the brain chemical serotonin."

So, they're basically saying if you *want* to be a dumb-dumb, don't eat carbs or anything in this book. But put differently, one could say this book might just "make you smarter, and happier."

And I'm okay with that.

Some Simple Ground Rules Before I Can Say Go:

- Read all the way through a recipe before attempting. There's nothing crazy in any of them, but like the Boy Scouts, you should be prepared.
- Whenever I say "oil," I mean a plain neutral oil—nothing flavored. Avocado oil, with its clean taste and high smoke point, is ideal. If I mean flavored oil, I'll say it.
- Salt means kosher salt because it's way better than table salt and less expensive for everyday use than sea salt. By the way, some d-bag once made a comment that kosher salt was only for Jews, which might be true . . . assuming Jews were the only people who cared about great-tasting food.
- Use more heat than you normally would, and I think you'll like the outcome. There are only a few things that don't benefit from more heat—and right now I can only think of scrambled eggs.
- You can upgrade everything in this book with a fried egg, caramelized onions, or crispy onions. Think of it: a sandwich, burger, burrito—they just all get better!
- Try something you normally wouldn't try once a month. Seriously, I'm not asking a lot. And my pushing you to try something new is not a bad thing either. The worst thing that happens is you end up learning and maybe liking more recipes, and that's good.

TACOS

Shortly after we opened Not Not Tacos (NNT), we got a Yelp review from a woman who said, and I quote, "You're making a mockery of the Mexican people by not serving Mexican tacos."

Ya gotta love people. San Diego has amazing Mexican food, plus the best Mexican food in the world is only 20 minutes from downtown San Diego—in real Mexico! And the last thing needed was more Mexican-inspired tacos, especially from a Jewish Canadian guy. So, I made tacos with unusual fillings, unusual at least for tacos.

And that's what ultimately inspired the name. Because as we described our taco fillings as Korean Short Rib, Pulled Pork with Mac and Cheese, Pastrami, Meatloaf, etc., people would ask, "Well, are they tacos or aren't they?" And Katie, a genius part of our group, said, "Well, they're not *not* tacos"—and it stuck.

The point is that anything in a tortilla can be a taco. And while Not Not doesn't have any Mexican-influenced tacos, this book does: you're gonna love my versions of Carne Asada and the Beef Birria (pages 24 and 49).

Oh—and if the cranky Yelp lady hated non-Mexican tacos, she's gonna really be pissed at my Orange Chicken Burrito (page 173), which we think of as our extremely delicious and positive version of cultural appropriation.

TORTILLAS: FLOUR, CORN, OR . . .

This is a debate that could literally fill this entire book. At NNT, we use *only* flour tortillas. And that's because I feel the aroma of a corn tortilla is so strong that when you lift a filled corn tortilla–wrapped taco up to your mouth, most of the time you smell only the corn tortilla. At Not Not, I want you to smell what's inside: the Korean short rib, the pastrami. or the Chinese cashew chicken. But it's really up to you and you should use whatever you want. And in the spirit of fairness, here are recipes for both flour and corn. And buying them already made is totally respectable, so don't let the tortilla police tell you it isn't. Last thing—if you're going to buy flour tortillas, look for the uncooked ones; they're really so much better.

NOTE: All tacos are assumed to be made on a 6-inch tortilla—corn or flour is up to you.

FLOUR TORTILLAS

MAKES ABOUT 18 TORTILLAS

4 cups all-purpose flour, plus more for dusting

1½ teaspoons salt

1⅔ to 2 cups warm water

¼ cup vegetable oil

NOTE: By the way, a fresh flour tortilla with only a little butter and a hint of kosher salt is life changing.

1. Put the flour and salt in a large bowl and whisk to combine well.
2. Add the water and oil. Using a wooden spoon, mix until dough starts to come together.
3. Now use your hands to turn it into a ball.
4. The dough should be sort of like Play-Doh (if you remember Play-Doh), so if it's too sticky, add a little flour about a tablespoon at a time. If it's too dry, add warm water a tablespoon at a time.
5. Dust your work surface with a little flour, take the dough out of the bowl, and knead for a couple of minutes until smooth.
6. Divide into 16 equal pieces, roll each into a ball, flour each one lightly, then set aside, cover with a kitchen towel, and let rest for 15 to 30 minutes.
7. Heat a large nonstick pan over medium-high heat.
8. Put each ball between two sheets of plastic wrap and either use a tortilla press or flatten into about a 6-inch round.
9. Gently put the tortilla into the pan and cook it for about 1 minute (you're waiting for a few golden-brown spots), then flip and cook for another 30 to 45 seconds.
10. Put the cooked tortilla in a clean, folded kitchen towel or tortilla warmer to keep warm.
11. Repeat with the remaining tortillas.

(CONTINUED)

CORN TORTILLAS

MAKES 16 TORTILLAS

2 cups masa harina (corn flour)
1 teaspoon salt
1½ to 2 cups warm water

NOTE: If the dough
sticks to your hands
and feels a little wet,
add a little more flour
a tablespoon or so
at a time. But if it
feels dry, add an extra
tablespoon or two of
hot water—you'll get it
down, trust me.

1. Combine the masa harina and salt in a large bowl, mix well, and add 1½ cups of the water.

2. Mix well, then knead with your hands until you get a soft dough.

3. Wrap the dough ball in plastic wrap and set aside about 30 minutes.

4. Cut the large ball into 16 pieces, roll each into a ball, place between two sheets of plastic wrap, and either use a tortilla press or flatten out into a 6-inch round.

5. Heat an ungreased cast-iron griddle or pan or a large nonstick pan over medium-high heat.

6. Gently lay one of the tortillas into the pan and cook for a minute or so on each side until lightly browned.

7. Repeat with the remaining tortillas.

Other Options

Your options for noncarb or non-animal-fat tortillas are pretty good these days. Of course, corn tortillas don't have any animal fat, but they have carbs. And apart from what's available in stores, such as cauliflower, coconut, and even egg white wraps, there's always leaves—not to mention they can be pretty damn delicious, too. You can use anything you like, but butter, Bibb, and Boston lettuce are great options. Romaine is a tad narrow, but still works and delivers a great crunch. And even the much-maligned iceberg lettuce (a fave of mine, by the way) is an excellent choice. I'd prob stay away from the cute little endive and radicchio, though, because they tend to be bitter. Oh, and another option can be thin slices of jicama—best cut with a mandoline to get them superthin.

How to Warm Tortillas

- In a nonstick pan over medium-high heat, a flour tortilla could take as little as 30 seconds a side.
- Over an open flame on your stove—keep flipping.
- On a hot grill—keep flipping.
- In a toaster—just don't let it get too crisp.
- In a microwave—don't even think of it.

YOUR FAVORITE LEFTOVER PROTEIN BREAKFAST TACO

Don't be fooled into thinking "breakfast" taco means you have to have it for breakfast. Because this is easily an "any time of day" thing in our family. And if you're just getting into the taco-making world, this is a great place to start because it happens so quickly.

MAKES 2 TACOS

1 tablespoon oil

2 tablespoons diced onion—red, yellow, or white up to you, Sparky

2 tablespoons sliced mushrooms

2 tablespoons seeded and diced green, red, or yellow pepper

⅓ cup of your favorite protein—cooked bacon, leftover carne asada, cooked chorizo, leftover chicken, cut-up hot dogs (don't laugh), literally anything

6 cooked leftover Homemade Tots (page 202) or a small handful of leftover fries cut into smaller pieces

2 large eggs, beaten

3 tablespoons shredded Monterey Jack

Pinch of kosher salt

2 warmed tortillas

Chipotle Lime Sour Cream (page 229)

Diced green onions for garnish (optional)

1. In a small nonstick pan over medium-high heat, add the oil, onion, mushrooms, and bell pepper. Cook until softened, about 3 minutes.

2. Add your protein and tots, stir well to combine, and cook until heated through, about 2 minutes.

3. Lower the heat slightly, add the eggs, cheese, and salt, and stir often to keep the eggs soft and prevent them from burning on the bottom.

4. Take your warm tortillas and to each add some of the chipotle cream and half of the filling, then top with green onions (if using).

5. Serve and rejoice.

SPICY HOISIN SALMON TACO

I tell people all the time that a variety of condiments from other countries can make a huge difference: Japanese mayo, Korean pepper paste, German curry ketchup, etc.—and this is the perfect example. While hoisin (think Chinese BBQ sauce) and chili paste are not hard to find, they will both do wonders for your eating.

MAKES 2 TACOS

4 green onions, white and light green parts only, sliced into thin shreds, plus more for garnish (optional)

¼ cup thinly shredded jicama

1 tablespoon mayonnaise

3 tablespoons hoisin sauce

1½ teaspoons Asian chili paste

1 tablespoon oil

One 4-ounce salmon fillet, without the skin, cut into 2 rectangular pieces

Kosher salt and freshly ground black pepper

2 warm tortillas

1. Combine the green onions, jicama, and mayo in a medium bowl, mix well to form a slaw, and set aside.

2. Mix the hoisin with the chili paste in a small bowl to make a sauce and set aside.

3. Heat the oil in a nonstick pan over medium-high heat, season the salmon with salt and pepper, and then put it into the pan.

4. Cook the salmon until you see it's cooked about one-third of the way up the side, then turn it over and repeat—this will keep the center a perfect tender.

5. Spread some sauce on each tortilla, add the slaw, top with the salmon, and finally garnish with the green onions (if using—and why the hell wouldn't you be?).

NOTE: If you prefer, feel free to grill the salmon until the same doneness.

GRILLED ASIAN CHICKEN TACO

I don't think chicken tacos get enough love, and I don't know why. Shrimp and carne asada are always the stars . . . but chicken? Honestly, I'm hoping this recipe can help change that.

MAKES 6 TACOS

¼ cup + 2 tablespoons Sambal chili sauce

2 tablespoons honey

1 tablespoon soy sauce

1 tablespoon oil

1½ teaspoons minced fresh ginger

2 garlic cloves, minced

3 boneless, skinless chicken thighs (yes, of course you can use breasts, but don't)

¼ cup sour cream or nonfat Greek yogurt

Cooking spray

6 tortillas

⅓ cup shredded cabbage—red or green doesn't matter

Chopped fresh cilantro for garnish

1. Combine ¼ cup of the chili sauce with the honey, soy sauce, oil, ginger, and garlic in a medium bowl and mix well.

2. Transfer about one-third of that mixture to a small bowl and refrigerate.

3. Then put the chicken and the rest of the chili sauce mixture in a zippered plastic bag to marinate, refrigerated, for a couple of hours up to overnight.

4. Combine the sour cream with the remaining 2 tablespoons of chili sauce, mix well and refrigerate.

5. Remove the chicken from the fridge about 30 minutes before cooking.

6. Heat the grill or a grill pan to high, spray with cooking spray, and put on the chicken, discarding its marinade.

7. Cook until well marked on both sides and cooked through, brushing it with the reserved chili sauce mixture as it cooks.

8. Remove the chicken from the grill, then thinly slice it.

9. Spread some of the sour cream sauce on a warm tortilla, add the cabbage and chicken, and garnish with a little chopped cilantro.

CARNE ASADA TACO

I don't think any taco I've ever done has received more love AND hate than this little guy—and for one, single, simple reason: the addition of the soy sauce. Let me start by saying that this carne asada is crazy delicious, but the soy sauce seems to have people freaked. Can't tell you how many people have shared that if their *"Mexican grandmother knew about this, she'd come talk sense into me."* All I can say is bring on the *abuelas*—I can handle them.

PROBABLY MAKES 10 TACOS

1 bunch cilantro, finely chopped, plus some for serving

3 large garlic cloves, minced

1 tablespoon ground cumin

1 tablespoon light brown sugar

½ cup oil

2 tablespoons soy sauce

Zest and juice of 1 lime

1 teaspoon kosher salt

1 teaspoon freshly ground black pepper

2 pounds skirt, flap, or flank steak (I prefer skirt and flap)

Warmed tortillas

Guacamole (page 230)

1 medium tomato, diced small

½ white or yellow onion, diced small

1. Combine the cilantro, garlic, cumin, brown sugar, oil, soy sauce, lime zest and juice, and the salt and pepper in a large bowl and mix well to create your marinade.

2. Put the marinade and the steak into a large zippered bag and seal, squeezing out as much air as possible, then squish around really well to make sure the steak is well covered. Refrigerate for 1 to 4 hours.

3. Remove the steak from fridge 30 to 45 minutes before cooking.

4. Heat a grill to high and grill the steak for about 3 minutes on each side or as necessary until it has an internal temperature of about 130°F or is done to your liking—and pardon me for butting in, but "your liking" should be 130°F.

5. Remove from the grill, cover with foil, and let rest for about 10 minutes before slicing thinly across the grain.

6. Heat the tortillas, then add some guacamole, the sliced carne, some of the tomato and onion, and finally a little garnish of cilantro.

GRILLED PORK AND PINEAPPLE TACO

Country-style pork ribs are one of my favorite things to grill; I just love them. And with this combo of spices and the pineapple, they get close to those crazy delicious al pastor tacos.

MAKES 4 TO 6 TACOS

1 tablespoon smoked paprika

1 tablespoon chipotle chile powder

1 tablespoon celery salt

1 tablespoon garlic powder

1 tablespoon onion powder

1 teaspoon kosher salt

½ teaspoon freshly ground black pepper

2 tablespoons light brown sugar

1 pound boneless country-style pork ribs

Two ½-inch-thick slices fresh pineapple

Neutral oil

3 tablespoons sour cream

Tortillas

2 tablespoons roughly chopped fresh cilantro

1. Mix together the paprika, chipotle chile powder, celery salt, garlic powder, onion powder, salt, pepper, and brown sugar in a small bowl to make the dry rub. Set aside.

2. Brush the pork with a little oil on all sides and sprinkle all over with the rub mixture, reserving at least a tablespoon of the rub mixture (you will have some left over).

3. Preheat the grill on medium-high, and cook the pork, turning often until you hit an internal temp of 145°F. Should take 10 to 15 minutes.

4. While the pork cooks, brush the pineapple with some oil and cook on the grill a couple of minutes per side or until well marked.

5. Remove the pork and pineapple from the grill.

6. Thinly slice the pork and dice the pineapple into bite-size pieces.

7. Mix the sour cream with about 1½ teaspoons of the remaining rub mixture.

8. Warm or cook the tortillas in a nonstick skillet.

9. Build: tortilla, sour cream, pork, pineapple, then top with cilantro.

FRESH TUNA WITH MANGO TACO

This is one of the first tacos I ever cooked, and it's still a fave. And even though there's nothing revolutionary about it—it's seriously a match made in food heaven.

MAKES 6 TO 8 TACOS

1 ripe mango, seeded, peeled, and diced small

2 tablespoons finely diced red onion

2 tablespoons chopped fresh cilantro

½ jalapeño pepper, seeded and finely chopped

Zest and juice of ½ fresh lime

Kosher salt

1 teaspoon chili powder

1 teaspoon garlic powder

1 teaspoon ground cumin

½ teaspoon kosher salt

Oil

1 pound uncooked fresh tuna, diced medium

Warmed tortillas

⅓ cup sour cream

Thinly shredded red cabbage

1. Combine the mango, onion, cilantro, jalapeño, lime zest and juice, and ¼ teaspoon of salt. Mix well and set the salsa aside (the flavor just gets better with time, so feel free to do this the day before).

2. Mix together the chili powder, garlic powder, cumin, and kosher salt to taste in a small bowl.

3. Lightly oil the tuna and season with some of the chili mixture.

4. In a nonstick pan over medium-high heat, add a tablespoon of oil and when almost smoking, add the tuna.

5. Sauté quickly, being careful not to break the tuna, and when almost done, sprinkle in a little more of the chili mixture and remove from the heat.

6. To the tortillas, add some sour cream, cabbage, tuna, and top with the mango salsa.

RED SNAPPER TACO

Here's the deal: this could also easily be halibut or even sea bass, but they're both pretty darn expensive. Go for it if you want, Elon, but snapper will be no less delicious and much easier on your wallet. Plus, you'll have money left over to add more Doge to your portfolio.

MAKES 6 TO 8 TACOS

1½ teaspoons oil

½ yellow onion, sliced thinly

1 pound red snapper, cut into 1-inch pieces

1½ teaspoons Old Bay seasoning

Juice of 1 lime

Tortillas

¼ cup sour cream

½ cup thinly shredded red cabbage

¼ cup green salsa

2 tablespoons diced green onions

1. In a nonstick pan over medium heat, add the oil and onion. Cook for about 5 minutes, or until nicely softened.

2. Add the snapper and Old Bay, and sauté until just cooked through—it won't take long, probably less than 5 minutes.

3. Add the lime juice, then stir and sauté for another minute. Remove from the pan.

4. Warm the tortillas in a nonstick skillet.

5. Spread a little sour cream on a warmed tortilla, add a little cabbage and some of the fish, and top it off with salsa and a sprinkle of green onion.

CRISPY SHRIMP TACO

Stop whatever you're doing and listen to me: however many shrimp you think you'll need for the tacos, make more, way more. Because when they start coming out of the oil, you'll be like "one for the tacos, one for me . . . one for the tacos, one for me." Understand?

MAKES 6 TACOS

Oil for frying

½ cup nonfat Greek yogurt or sour cream

1 to 2 tablespoons minced chipotle chile

Juice of ¼ lime

1 cup all-purpose flour

1 teaspoon kosher salt

1 teaspoon garlic powder

1 teaspoon chipotle or regular chili powder

2 large eggs, beaten

2 cups panko bread crumbs

8 ounces 31/40 raw shrimp, peeled and deveined with tails removed

Tortillas

2 cups shredded green cabbage

1. Preheat about an inch of oil in a medium pot to 350°F.

2. Combine the yogurt with the chipotle and lime juice in a small bowl.

3. Put the flour in a medium bowl with the salt, garlic powder, and chili powder, and mix well.

4. Put the beaten eggs in a separate bowl, and the panko in yet another bowl.

5. Prep the shrimp: dust them with the flour mixture (shaking off the excess), dip them well into the egg to coat, coat well in the panko to cover, and finally transfer to a plate.

6. When the oil is hot enough, gently—and I mean gently—place the shrimp in the oil, not overcrowding the pot to keep the temperature from going down too much.

7. Cook for 2 to 2½ minutes, turning them halfway during that time if they're not submerged, or until golden brown, and then transfer to paper towels to drain.

8. Build your tacos: tortilla, some of the chipotle sauce, cabbage, and shrimp.

KOREAN SHORT RIB TACO

The day we opened Not Not Tacos in 2018, this became the #1 taco and has never been dethroned. Oh, and this may seem like a bunch of ingredients, but it's good . . . it's really damn good.

MAKES 6 TACOS

1 pound boneless short rib, cut across the grain into very thin slices (by the way, it's easier if you put it into the freezer for about 45 minutes first)

¾ cup Marinade (recipe follows)

Oil for frying

6 tortillas

⅓ cup Gochujang Sauce (recipe follows)

⅓ cup sour cream

⅓ cup thinly shredded jicama

2 tablespoons Crispy Panko (recipe follows)

¼ cup finely diced green onion

1. Combine the sliced short rib with the marinade in a shallow bowl or zippered bag, combine to make sure everything is well coated, and refrigerate for 1 to 2 hours or overnight.

2. Heat a large skillet, pan, or wok over high heat.

3. When it's almost smoking, add a splash of oil and the marinated short rib (discard the remaining marinade).

4. Stir quickly—because it's thin, it'll cook pretty fast, like in about a minute.

5. Warm the tortillas and build: tortilla, gochujang sauce, and sour cream on the tortilla, then some jicama, the short rib, and finally the panko and green onion.

MARINADE

MAKES ABOUT ½ CUP

⅓ cup soy sauce

2 tablespoons honey

2 tablespoons light brown sugar

1½ tablespoons sesame oil

2 garlic cloves, minced

One 1-inch piece fresh ginger, finely chopped

4 green onions, cut into 1-inch pieces

Put everything in a processor or blender and whiz away until well mixed.

(CONTINUED)

GOCHUJANG SAUCE

MAKES ABOUT ⅓ CUP

2 tablespoons gochujang
  (see note)

3 tablespoons low-fat sour cream

2 teaspoons rice vinegar

¼ teaspoon toasted sesame oil

Combine all the ingredients in a bowl, mix well, and refrigerate until needed.

NOTE: Gochujang is Korean red chile pepper paste that's quickly becoming available at many supermarkets. If not where you are, then online for sure. Once you have it, check my website for other recipes with it, because it's awesome.

CRISPY PANKO

MAKES ABOUT 1 CUP

1½ tablespoons salted butter

1 cup panko bread crumbs

1. Melt the butter in a small pan and add the panko.

2. Stir until the panko has sucked up all the butter (I couldn't think of a better way to say that) and has turned a beautiful golden color, then remove from the heat and set aside.

NOTE: I'm not saying this is the key to the taco, but the textural component it adds is so dang important.

SAN DIEGO FISH TACO

As a San Diegan, if I eff this up, there's a good chance they'll ask me to leave the city . . . forever. And that's because the fish taco is pretty much the most iconic thing you can eat here. But if you've never had one, I'll admit a fish taco can sound a bit, oh . . . gross, actually. But honestly, that couldn't be further from the truth. Guess the only way you'll find out is to make them.

MAKES 6 TACOS

¾ cup sour cream

⅓ cup green salsa

1 cup dry tempura batter

1 tablespoon Old Bay seasoning

¾ cup Mexican beer, or soda water, or the beer—yeah, it should be the beer

Oil for frying

1¼ pounds white fish (cod, halibut, mahi-mahi), skinned, deboned, patted dry, and sliced into finger-size pieces, approximately 1 by 3 inches

Kosher salt and freshly ground black pepper

1 cup all-purpose flour

6 tortillas

¾ cup thinly sliced green cabbage

Hot sauce and lime wedges for serving

1. Combine the sour cream and salsa in a small bowl, mix well, and set aside.

2. Combine the tempura batter and Old Bay with the beer in a large bowl and whisk together until smooth.

3. Heat a couple of inches of oil to 360°F in a deep-sided pan or pot.

4. Season both sides of the fish with salt and pepper and coat with the flour, shaking off any excess.

5. Dip the fish into the batter, gently shake off any excess, then fry in batches in the oil until golden brown and cooked through—about 5 minutes, or until beautifully golden brown (don't overcrowd the pot of oil or the temp will drop, it won't cook properly, and you'll be pissed at me).

6. Transfer to paper towels to drain and repeat with the remaining fish.

7. Warm the tortillas and build your tacos: to each tortilla add some of the sour cream sauce, cabbage, a piece or two of the fish, and then a drizzle of hot sauce and a squeeze of lime juice.

NASHVILLE HOT CHICKEN TACO

Yes, there's also more than a handful of ingredients in this one, too, but it is what it is. You need spark plugs, a battery, four tires, and a transmission to drive a car, and you need all this for the taco. If it's too much, come to Not Not Tacos . . . we'll be happy to sell you a few.

MAKES 6 TACOS

Brined Chicken (recipe follows)

6 ounces mixed coleslaw
  or shredded cabbage
  (any color will work)

¼ cup good mayonnaise

2 teaspoons cider vinegar

Pinch of kosher salt

⅛ teaspoon freshly
  ground black pepper

Oil for frying

Hot Oil Sauce (recipe follows)

Flour Dredge (recipe follows)

6 tortillas

6 dill pickle planks

1. Prepare the brined chicken.

2. When ready to cook, combine the coleslaw with the mayo, vinegar, salt, and pepper in a medium nonreactive bowl—mix well and refrigerate.

3. Heat at least an inch of oil in a large skillet to 360°F.

4. Prepare the hot oil sauce—we'll be coming back to this at the end.

5. Prepare the flour dredge.

6. Remove the chicken pieces from the buttermilk, letting any excess drip off, then put them into the flour dredge, shake off excess, then back into the buttermilk, and finally into the flour again, making sure that the chicken is really well coated.

7. Shake off any excess flour and put on a plate or baking sheet. Repeat with all the chicken.

8. Slowly add the coated chicken to the oil, being careful not to overcrowd the skillet—you might need to do this in two batches—and cook until golden brown and crisp on both sides (turning the pieces over about halfway if using a pan) until the chicken reaches an internal temp of 160 to 165°F (remember these are thighs, so longer for breasts).

9. If making a couple batches, move the cooked pieces to a rack-covered baking sheet and put in a 250°F oven while you finish the rest.

10. When all the frying is done, very carefully add about 1 cup of the hot cooking oil to the pot with the spices to prepare the hot oil sauce—stir superwell to combine.

11. Remove the chicken from the oven and brush both sides of each piece well with the hot oil sauce.

12. Add some slaw to a tortilla, then the chicken, and finally top with a pickle plank.

(CONTINUED)

BRINED CHICKEN

MAKES 6 PIECES

3 cups buttermilk

2 tablespoons hot sauce (I'm a fan of Cholula, but any will do)

1 tablespoon smoked paprika

1 teaspoon kosher salt

½ teaspoon freshly ground black pepper

3 large chicken thighs, sliced in half lengthwise (you can use breasts, but if you're asking, I'd go with thighs)

1. Combine the brine ingredients in a large bowl, whisk well, and add the chicken.

2. Make sure it's all well covered and refrigerate for 4 hours or ideally overnight.

HOT OIL SAUCE

MAKES 1 CUP

¼ cup cayenne pepper

2 tablespoons light brown sugar

1 tablespoon garlic powder

1 tablespoon smoked paprika (regular is fine)

1 tablespoon chipotle chile powder (regular is fine)

1 teaspoon red pepper flakes

Put everything in a large, heatproof bowl and whisk together. After frying the chicken, add 1 cup of the hot cooking oil to the bowl and stir well to combine.

FLOUR DREDGE

MAKES ABOUT 2 CUPS

1 cup all-purpose flour

1 cup cornstarch

1 tablespoon smoked paprika

1 tablespoon kosher salt

1 teaspoon freshly ground black pepper

Put everything in a large bowl and whisk together until combined.

LAMB TACO

This is one of the tacos I made for our Not Not team during testing before we opened. Everyone loved it, but much to my dismay, it didn't make the final menu—I felt eight of their opinions outweighed one of mine. But about six months after we opened, I made it again for everyone to taste and proposed it as a monthly special. They ate, thought it was so good, and wondered why it wasn't on the permanent menu. Geez, some people's kids. By the way, it's a permanent member now.

MAKES 5 OR 6 TACOS

Oil
Marinated lamb (recipe follows)
Tortillas
Tzatziki (recipe follows)
Parsley Tomato Salad
  (recipe follows)
Parsley for garnish

1. In a nonstick pan over high heat, add a splash of oil and then some of the marinated lamb.

2. Stir constantly, as it will cook very fast, and as soon as it loses its pinkish hue, it's done—about a minute.

3. Warm a tortilla, add some tzatziki, the lamb, some parsley tomato salad, and finally garnish with a little more parsley.

MARINATED LAMB

MAKES 1 POUND

⅓ cup soy sauce
½ teaspoon red pepper flakes
Juice of ½ lemon
1 teaspoon ground cumin
2 garlic cloves, minced
¼ small red onion, sliced thinly
Kosher salt and freshly
  ground black pepper
1 pound thinly sliced lamb

1. Put all the ingredients, except the lamb, in a large bowl, mix well, then add the lamb.

2. Make sure it's well coated, then cover and refrigerate for a few hours or overnight.

(CONTINUED)

TZATZIKI

MAKES ABOUT 1 CUP

½ cup Greek yogurt

⅓ cup finely diced cucumber, squeezed in a clean kitchen towel to remove excess moisture

1 large garlic clove, minced

1 tablespoon finely chopped fresh dill

1 lemon wedge

Kosher salt

Combine everything in a bowl, mix well, and refrigerate.

PARSLEY TOMATO SALAD

MAKES ABOUT 1½ CUPS

2 medium vine-ripened tomatoes, seeded and diced small

½ small red onion, finely diced

2 Persian cucumbers or ½ small English cucumber, diced small

1 tablespoon olive oil

2 tablespoons red wine vinegar

¼ cup chopped fresh parsley

½ teaspoon kosher salt

Put all the ingredients in a large bowl and mix well to combine, then refrigerate.

PORK AND MAC TACO

When we were in the tasting phase before opening Not Not Tacos, I would have six or seven from our group over and make the tacos I was proposing for the menu. One day as we were wrapping up, Jon, one of my partners, asked whether I could do anything with macaroni and cheese. The next time we all got together, I busted out this kid, and the rest is delicious pork and mac history. So, Jon gets credit for suggesting mac, just not the whole damn taco.

MAKES 6 TACOS

2 cups dried elbow macaroni

¾ cup Cheez Whiz

⅓ cup shredded Monterey Jack

1 tablespoon pork rub, store-bought is fine or see recipe that follows

1½ teaspoons salted butter

1 cup diced yellow onion

Tortillas

Sour cream

12 ounces leftover or store-bought pulled pork (by the way, a supereasy recipe for Kalua Pork is in my book *Recipes with Intentional Leftovers* and would be ideal here)

Sriracha and diced green onions for garnish

1. Boil a large pot of water and add the macaroni—immediately stir to prevent sticking and cook for about 8 minutes, or until just done. Drain, reserving ½ cup of the pasta water.

2. Return the pasta to the pot. Add the Cheez Whiz, Monterey Jack, pork rub, and mix well to combine, adding as much of the reserved pasta water as necessary to make it creamy, but not too creamy because it needs to stay on the taco.

3. Meanwhile, as the macaroni cooks, melt the butter in a nonstick pan over medium heat, add the diced onion, and cook until translucent, 4 to 5 minutes, then remove from the heat and set aside.

4. Warm the tortillas and build your taco: spread some sour cream down the middle of a tortilla, add about a tablespoon or so of the sautéed onion, then some pork, some mac, a drizzle of sriracha, and finally a sprinkling of green onions.

PORK RUB

MAKES ABOUT 1 CUP

¼ cup light brown sugar

¼ cup kosher salt

2 tablespoons smoked paprika

1 tablespoon coarsely ground black pepper

1 teaspoon ground cumin

1 teaspoon chili powder

1 teaspoon onion powder

1 teaspoon garlic powder

½ teaspoon cayenne pepper

Combine everything in a bowl, mix well, and seal in something with a tight-fitting lid.

BEEF BIRRIA TACO

This is deeply flavored, supertender beef, finished on a flat top along with melty cheese and some of the leftover stock for steaming. We made this for YouTube and it was an instant success, and for good reason—it's just crazy addictive. Yes, it can take a bit in the oven, so I've added pressure cooker instructions, too. But no matter what version you make, you're gonna be like, "Oh, holy crap, I'm in love." Oh, the chiles are easily ordered online if you can't find them locally. One last thing—this shredded beef . . . the next day . . . just in some scrambled eggs—is OMG amazing!

MAKES A LOT; OKAY, MAYBE A DOZEN OR SO

4 dried guajillo chiles, stemmed and seeded

2 dried pasilla chiles, stemmed and seeded

2 cups boiling beef stock (chicken is absolutely okay, too)

1 tablespoon dried oregano

1 teaspoon ground cumin

2 teaspoons ground coriander

2 chipotle chiles (the type in adobo sauce)

Kosher salt and freshly ground black pepper

One 15-ounce can diced fire-roasted tomatoes

3 pounds boneless short ribs

Oil for cooking

1 yellow onion

6 garlic cloves, minced

3 tablespoons cider vinegar

For serving:

Corn tortillas

Shredded Monterey Jack

Diced white onion

Chopped fresh cilantro

1. Preheat the oven to 350°F (if not using a pressure cooker).

2. Put the stemmed and seeded guajillo and pasilla chiles into a blender, add the boiling stock, cover, and let sit for 5 minutes.

3. Add the oregano, cumin, coriander, chipotles, salt and black pepper to taste, and the diced tomatoes. Blend until smooth.

4. Brush the short ribs lightly with oil, season well with salt and black pepper, and sear half the beef in an ovenproof pot with a tight-fitting lid over medium-high heat. Transfer to a plate and repeat with the remaining beef. If using a pressure cooker, set to BROWNING and do the exact same thing.

5. To either empty pot, now add the onion and garlic with a little more oil and cook until softened, about 5 minutes.

6. Add the vinegar, scraping up the bits on the bottom, and allow about half of the vinegar to evaporate, then add back the beef and remove from the heat.

7. Pour the chile mixture over the beef in the pot—the beef should be covered, and if not, add a little more stock.

8. Cover and place in the oven to roast until fork-tender and shreddable, 2½ to 3 hours. If using a pressure cooker: seal and set to high pressure for 55 minutes, then allow the pressure to release. For both, when done, remove the pieces of beef and shred . . . it's so good.

9. To make the tacos: dip a tortilla into some of the leftover cooking liquid and place on a flat top or nonstick pan.

10. When it starts to get a little browned, flip it over and add some shredded cheese, some beef, a little more cheese, and fold over.

11. Drizzle a little of the chile-flavored stock on top and cook until it gets crispy on both sides.

12. Remove, open up carefully, add onion and cilantro, and eat.

MANGO DESSERT TACO

My brother-in-law Brian (who's not really a dessert fan) asks for these tacos almost everytime I see him. And because these taste like summer with the mango and the ice cream, you should definitely try grilling the tortillas on your barbecue instead of cooking them in a pan.

MAKES 6 TO 8 TACOS

¼ cup sugar

2 teaspoons ground cinnamon

Flour tortillas

Salted butter

About 1½ cups vanilla ice cream (it should be a really good vanilla)

2 fresh mangoes, peeled and diced

Hot honey (as in spicy, not temperature!)

½ lemon

Powdered sugar

1. Combine the sugar and cinnamon in a small bowl.

2. Brush both sides of the tortilla lightly with butter and sprinkle well with cinny-sugar.

3. Cook in a nonstick pan over medium heat until slightly crispy and browned on both sides, about 1 minute or so per side, then transfer to a serving plate.

4. Add ice cream to each tortilla and top with mango.

5. Drizzle with honey, a squeeze of lemon. and then a sprinkle of powdered sugar.

BURGERS

As I think of it, burgers could literally be the perfect handheld meal. Carbs, protein, veggies, dairy, sauce—I mean, what else combines all these elements in an easy-to-eat and fricking delicious package?

We started our burger restaurant out of necessity, no seriously. Our restaurant group had leased a large location, and even before we got the keys . . . the pandemic hit. And since it didn't look like anyone could go into any restaurant for at least the foreseeable future, we thought it would be a good idea to open up a burger spot for takeout and delivery, and Samburgers was born—damn, I love that name. And since burgers were also so popular on my YouTube channel, it seemed like a no-brainer.

A good burger is one of those foods everyone should be able to make. It's right up there with an omelet, a perfect medium-rare steak, and a damn fine grilled cheese—golden brown, crispy, gooey, a fantastic cheese pull, and crazy delicious (garlic mayo on the outside is the key here, by the way).

And so this chapter will cover thick burgers, smashed burgers, stuffed burgers, and even one with a beer can shoved into it—yes, it's a thing. We'll also scope out my fave burger blend, other grind options, and, of course, toppings (including a most delicious bacon-onion jam), and of course, what to serve your burger on.

That's all good and well, but we've gotta get happening—so start reading and then get ready to start cooking; this is gonna be great.

It's a Grind

Beef is sold by its "lean-to-fat ratio"—for example, 95/5 means it's a combination of 95 percent lean and 5 percent fat. But the expression *fat means flavor* was never more important than right here. So, for our purposes, the only thing you should reach for is 80/20. And before you freak out that it's too much fat—it's not. The burger will be rich and delicious with the right amount of fat. IMO, it would be better to have a great burger once a month than a mediocre burger once a week. And if the 80/20 rule is the only thing you take away from this chapter, your burger world is going to be greatly elevated.

But now we come to the idea of grinding your own beef—or having it ground for you. And this, my friends, is literally a game changer. Imagine going from what is mostly one type of beef to two or three? The additional flavors that are going to show up will make for an insane bite or 10. But this can be a personal thing, and more types of beef are not necessarily better. At Samburgers, we use a combo of sirloin, brisket, and short rib—and our burgers are crazy good. And when cooking, they smell more like steak than ground beef. But it may take you a bit to figure out your preference, so I suggest you test drive a few combos.

If you want to commit to buying a grinder or a grinding attachment for a mixer, go for it. The other way is to find a butcher that'll grind for you—then simply choose a few cuts and see what you come up with. For simplicity's sake, I'll tell you that more than a few times I've combined ground sirloin 50/50 with only ground brisket (still maintaining the 20 percent fat ratio) and the burgers were nuts . . . in a good way.

So, if you're going to use a grinder, follow these simple rules:

- Start by cutting the meat into about 1½-inch cubes—it'll need to fit into the tube of the grinder.
- Make sure your meat is cold—once cut, put the cubes into the freezer (to get cold, not frozen) about 30 minutes before grinding. Warm meat can get mushy, and no one wants that.
- Once ground, shape into balls or patties—but be gentle and try to handle as little as possible. A tightly compacted patty will not be nearly as juicy as a less compacted one.

No grinder? No problem. A food processor can get you there. Follow the three rules above, and whatever you do, don't overcrowd and try to process everything at once or it will become a gross pile of red mush—too graphic? I'm saying less is more. And use the Pulse button about a second or two at a time until nicely chopped. This could take anywhere from 10 to 20 pulses.

How Big a Burger, Sam?

You really only need to know two different ways to cook a burger patty. And so for (almost) every burger in this book, you can do either:

QUARTER-POUND SMASHED: Arguably one of the best, simplest, and most delicious ways to go.

THIRD-POUND THICK: Juicy, gorgeous, and perfect.

There's a famous self-help book written in 1936 by Dale Carnegie called *How to Win Friends and Influence People*, which even today is on the 100 Most Influential Books list (spoiler alert: being nice is a big part of it). But here's the point: if these were the only two types of patties you knew how to cook, you could go anywhere in the world and become instantly popular, win friends, and influence people. So, any recipe in this chapter can be made with either the smashed or thick technique, unless I have strong feelings, at which point I'll tell you the one I think you should use. And here's how to cook them.

QUARTER-POUND SMASHED

1. Separate 4 ounces of ground beef and form it into a ball, then set aside.
2. Heat a griddle, grill pan, flat top, or cast-iron pan to high—about 500°F.
3. Add a little oil to your cooking surface and place the ball on top of the oil.
4. Using a large, wide spatula or two, press down on the ball until roughly ¼ inch thick, then season with salt and freshly ground black pepper.
5. Let cook for about a minute, then flip over. Because it's so thin, there's no need to season side two.
6. Oh, and if you're going to add cheese, now's the time.
7. Cook for another minute, then remove from the heat.

NOTE: This is easily turned into a double or even a triple with almost no more time or effort, and that's just wonderful.

THIRD-POUND THICK

1. Separate 5.3 ounces of ground beef and, using either a burger press (which frankly is kind of a waste of $$) or your hands (which are free and you never need to look for them), shape into a 4-inch-wide by almost 1-inch-thick patty. As long as you get the 4-inch part right, the thickness will handle itself.

2. Heat a griddle, grill pan, flat top, or cast-iron pan to medium-high—about 400 to 450°F.

3. Add a little oil to your cooking surface and place the patty on the oil. Season with salt and freshly ground black pepper.

4. Cook for 3 minutes, then flip over, season again, and feel free to add cheese at this point. And before you bitch me out for the cheese taking a minute on the smashed one and almost 3 minutes here—remember that the smashed, the cheese is way closer to the cooking surface.

5. Cook for another 2 to 3 minutes on this side, then remove from the heat.

What's in a Protein?

The last thing we need to discuss when it comes to a burger is what it's made of. We've covered beef and different beef grind combos, but I'd be negligent if I didn't mention other options . . .

CHICKEN: One of my favorites is a burger made from ground chicken thighs—and trust me, forget about using breasts. And this actually lends itself really well to being prepped in a processor—just remember to pulse.

SALMON: I save random pieces of salmon when I'm prepping it for dinner, then use those pieces for a patty the next day. And of any of the proteins, salmon can easily be prepped with a good knife instead of a machine. A little spicy teriyaki sauce and you're golden.

PORK: Easily an overlooked option, but why? Yes, ground pork needs some help in the flavor department, but it's still really good. Pork, the other burger.

PLANT BASED: There's a handful of very good plant options out there, and they can be the star of any burger. They look, act, feel, and depending which one, even taste like beef.

THE KEVIN BACON BURGER

Thick

Thank you to YouTube subscriber Guille, who turned us on to this from a burger chain in Spain.

MAKES 2 BURGERS

½ small yellow onion, diced

1 teaspoon oil, plus more for cooking the burger

1 teaspoon salted butter

6 strips uncooked bacon, chopped small

8 ounces ground beef or whatever

⅓ cup crispy french-fried onions or Crispy Onions (page 205)

Salt and freshly ground black pepper

2 slices white Cheddar

2 buns

¼ cup mayonnaise

1. Cook the onion in oil and butter in a pan over medium heat until softened, about 5 minutes.

2. In a separate pan, cook the bacon until about halfway done—remove half from the pan, set aside, and continue to cook the rest until almost crispy, then remove from the heat and drain on paper towels.

3. Combine the ground beef, softened onion, half-cooked bacon, and ¼ cup of the crispy onions in a bowl.

4. Season with salt and pepper and mix together well, then form into two patties.

5. Put 1 tablespoon or so of oil into a large skillet over medium heat, and when hot, add the patties.

6. Cook to your liking, then flip over and add the cheese.

7. Toast the buns, add mayo to both halves, and then add the cooked patties, rest of the crispy bacon, and the remaining crispy onions.

8. Eat!

JALAPEÑO AND GUACAMOLE BURGER

Smashed or Thick

The guac just adds beautifully to the big flavors and textures of this delicious burger.

MAKES 3 OR 4 BURGERS

1½ teaspoons salted butter

2 jalapeño peppers, sliced into ⅛-inch rings

8 ounces ground beef

8 ounces ground brisket

Salt and freshly ground black pepper

2 slices pepper Jack

Brioche buns, toasted

¼ cup mayonnaise

¼ cup Guacamole (page 230)

¼ cup crispy french-fried onions or Crispy Onions (page 205)

1. Melt the butter in a small skillet, add the jalapeños, and cook over medium heat until softened, about 5 minutes. Remove from the heat and set aside.

2. Combine the beef and brisket in a medium bowl, mix together gently, and shape into three or four patties.

3. Cook, seasoning with salt and pepper, and add the cheese when you flip.

4. Spread each bun bottom with mayo, add the patties with cheese, guacamole, jalapeños, crispy onions, and the bun top.

SALMON BURGER

Thick

For too many people a salmon burger is a quick no, and that's sad. We don't grow unless we push ourselves, and this is the moment (nicely dramatic, huh?). At the end of many YouTube videos, I say, "You've gotta make this." Guess what?

MAKES 2 BURGERS

Oil

1 red bell pepper, 4 sides cut off

8 ounces raw salmon, finely chopped

1 tablespoon fresh lemon juice

1½ teaspoons Dijon mustard

1 tablespoon capers

¼ cup mayonnaise

3 tablespoons panko bread crumbs

Kosher salt and freshly ground black pepper

1 tablespoon sriracha

2 tablespoons salted butter

2 burger buns

⅓ cup alfalfa sprouts

1. In a hot skillet over medium heat, heat 1 tablespoon of oil and add the bell pepper. Cook until well softened and charred in spots, about 5 minutes, then set aside.

2. Combine the salmon, lemon juice, Dijon, capers, 2 tablespoons of the mayo, panko, and a pinch each of salt and pepper in a bowl. Form into two patties, put on waxed or parchment paper, and refrigerate about 30 to 60 minutes.

3. Heat a skillet or flat griddle over medium heat, add about 1 tablespoon of oil, and when hot, cook the patties for about 3 minutes per side, or until golden and crispy.

4. While they cook, combine the remaining 2 tablespoons of mayo and the sriracha in a small bowl.

5. Butter and toast or grill the buns until golden.

6. Layer each bun bottom with the sriracha mixture, bell pepper, some sprouts, and a patty.

7. Add the bun top—eat!

THE LUTHER BURGER

Smashed or Thick

When we shoot for YouTube, Max often suggests what I should make, and one day he offered this "doughnut-in-place-of-buns" ridiculousness. Sometimes I go with his suggestions—I mean, he is younger and often has a better feel for what our audience will like—but sometimes I argue and suggest something else. And whether he caught me in a weak moment this time or what, I don't remember, but I relented. And pretty much the entire time I was making it, I fully assumed it would taste awful but would be great entertainment regardless. But I was wrong because it actually works—as in pretty damn good. It's that savory/sweet thing, and I'm still amazed . . .

MAKES 3 OR 4 BURGERS

2 tablespoons diced dill pickle

2 tablespoons mayonnaise

1 tablespoon ketchup

2 teaspoons whole-grain mustard

1 teaspoon minced chipotle chile

1 pound ground beef

1 tablespoon Montreal
  steak seasoning

American cheese slices

3 or 4 glazed doughnuts

Salted butter

3 or 4 large eggs

6 strips cooked bacon

1. Combine the pickle, mayo, ketchup, mustard, and chipotle chile in a small bowl, mix well to create a sauce, and set aside.

2. Combine the beef with the Montreal steak seasoning, form into patties, and cook.

3. When you flip the patties, add the cheese slices.

4. While the patties cook, slice the doughnuts in half, spread butter on the cut sides, and cook on a flat top or nonstick pan over medium heat until golden.

5. Fry the eggs in a little butter as well—don't break the yolk!

6. Build: add the sauce to each doughnut bottom, then layer with the patty, bacon, fried egg, and doughnut top.

EGGS BENNY BURGER

Smashed

"This is wrong," they said. "You can't do this," they said. Well, I don't know who "they" are, but why the eff not? Because for me, a lover of burgers *and* poached eggs, this is a dream . . . not to mention it has all the essential components of a proper Benedict.

MAKES 2 BURGERS

2 tablespoons mayonnaise
1 tablespoon sriracha
8 ounces hot Italian sausage
2 slices Muenster
6 slices deli Black Forest ham, sliced thinly
2 English muffins
Salted butter
2 Poached Eggs (recipe follows)
Hollandaise (recipe follows)
Minced chives for garnish

1. Combine the mayo with the sriracha in a small bowl, mix well, and set aside.

2. Form the sausage meat into two patties and cook on one side, then flip, add the cheese, and cook until done.

3. In a nonstick pan over medium heat, cook the ham until the edges are slightly crispy

4. Cut the English muffins in half, butter each inner side, and lightly toast or grill.

5. Build: on each muffin bottom, add the mayo mixture, patty, ham, poached egg, and hollandaise; garnish with chives; and add the muffin top.

POACHED EGG

MAKES 1 POACHED EGG

1 large egg
White vinegar

1. Bring a small pot of water to a low simmer (tiny bubbles breaking on the surface) and stir in the vinegar—the vinegar will help pull the egg white together.

2. Crack the egg into a small cup. Using a large spoon, swirl the simmering water in the pot to create a mini vortex, then lower the cup toward the center of the swirl almost touching the water, and gently slip the egg into the vortex—the egg will start coming together.

3. Using a slotted spoon, start checking at around 2½ minutes—the white should be set and the yolk soft.

4. When ready, use right away or immediately transfer the poached egg to a bowl of ice water—it'll keep perfectly in the water for a couple of days in the fridge. When you want to use it, bring a small pot of water to a simmer and slip in the egg to reheat for about a minute, then simply remove and use.

(CONTINUED)

HOLLANDAISE

MAKES ABOUT 1 CUP

10 tablespoons (1 stick +
   2 tablespoons) salted butter
3 large egg yolks
1 tablespoon fresh lemon juice
⅛ teaspoon cayenne pepper
Pinch of kosher salt

1. Melt the butter in a small pot over low heat; don't let it burn.

2. Combine the egg yolks, lemon juice, cayenne, and salt in a blender. Mix on medium speed for 30 to 60 seconds, until very pale yellow.

3. Reduce the blender speed to low and slowly drizzle in the melted butter until everything is mixed and thickened nicely.

4. Turn off the blender, taste, and use. To keep warm, pour into a thermos right away.

CHILI CHEESE BURGER

Smashed

This is truly an iconic combination, and if there were a Mount Rushmore of burgers, this simple little guy would be chiseled into the granite (and probably dripping down the granite, too). And while you can use whatever protein you want for the patty, I really think it needs to be beef or chicken.

MAKES 2 BURGERS

8 ounces ground beef, formed into 2 patties

Kosher salt and freshly ground black pepper

2 slices American cheese

Salted butter

2 burger buns

¼ cup Burger Sauce (page 228)

½ cup Burger/Hot Dog Chili (page 221)

½ cup Crispy Onions (page 205)

1. Heat a griddle, add the patties, season with salt and pepper, and cook.

2. Add the cheese when you flip them.

3. While they cook, butter the buns and toast or grill lightly, remove from the heat, and add burger sauce to each bun bottom.

4. Place a patty on the sauce, then add the chili, crispy onions, and bun top.

5. Serve . . . with lots of napkins.

JUICY LUCY BURGER

Thick

We're fans of regional food, and this is one very fun example of it. This cheese-stuffed burger hails from Minnesota and is probably the perfect thing on those subzero evenings . . . with a side of parka and an electric blanket.

MAKES 2 BURGERS

1 pound ground beef

1 tablespoon soy paste or regular soy sauce

1½ teaspoons garlic powder

Kosher salt and freshly ground black pepper

2 slices American cheese

2 buns

¼ cup mayonnaise

1 dill pickle, cut into ⅛-inch disks

1. Put the ground beef in a bowl and add the soy, garlic powder, salt, and pepper. Mix well, then separate into four balls.

2. On a large piece of parchment or waxed paper, flatten each ball into about a 4-inch-diameter patty.

3. Fold each slice of cheese into quarters, place a folded cheese stack on each of the two flattened patties, then top each with the remaining patty.

4. Carefully squeeze the edges together well to seal—you don't want the cheese leaking out.

5. Cook the patties over medium heat until cooked through, 3 to 4 minutes per side.

6. While they cook, toast the buns, and then build: bun bottom, mayo, pickles, patty, bun top.

LOCO MOCO BURGER

Thick

Think of this as Hawaii's version of Salisbury steak—except, if you're like me, Salisbury steak is something you mostly want to forget. But not so in this case, because this is easily one of the greatest things you can do with a hamburger patty.

MAKES 2 BURGERS

1 tablespoon salted butter

1 tablespoon oil

8 ounces cremini mushrooms, stems removed, thinly sliced

2 tablespoons vermouth or white wine (optional)

1 cup beef stock

1 tablespoon cornstarch

2 tablespoons water

10.6 ounces ground beef

¼ cup finely diced red onion

1 garlic clove, minced

1½ teaspoons soy paste or soy sauce

Kosher salt and freshly ground black pepper

For serving:

2 cups cooked, warm white rice

2 tablespoons finely diced green onion

2 large eggs, preferably sunny-side up or over-easy (it's all about the runny yolk)

1. Melt the butter with the oil in a medium nonstick pan and add the mushrooms. Cook over medium-high heat until softened, about 5 minutes.

2. If using the vermouth or wine (which you should be), add it now, but keep the pan off the flame so there's no chance of a flare-up. Then mix it in and cook until most has evaporated.

3. Add the beef stock and bring to a simmer.

4. Mix the cornstarch with the water in a cup until fully dissolved, stir into the mushrooms, continuing to stir until the liquid thickens. Then lower the heat and keep warm.

5. Combine the ground beef with the red onion, garlic, and soy paste in a bowl. Season well with salt and pepper and shape into two patties.

6. Heat your grill or griddle to medium-high and cook the patties.

7. While they cook, combine the rice with the green onion in a bowl and mix well.

8. Build: put the rice on each plate, add a patty, then some gravy, and finally top with a cooked egg.

SHRIMP SLIDERS

Yes, I realize this chapter is about burgers and this is a slider . . . but isn't a slider just a baby burger? The answer is yes, and therefore it can be made out of anything, but these shrimp guys hold a special place in my heart. Crispy, golden, with a touch of heat . . . I could eat all eight.

MAKES 8 SLIDERS

4 green onions, white and light green parts, roughly chopped

½ red bell pepper, seeded and roughly chopped

One ½-inch piece fresh ginger, roughly chopped

2 garlic cloves, peeled and smashed with the side of a knife

1 pound uncooked shrimp, peeled and deveined

¾ cup panko bread crumbs

6 tablespoons mayonnaise

2 teaspoons soy paste or soy sauce

1½ cups thinly shredded cabbage (napa cabbage would be great here)

1 tablespoon sriracha

1 tablespoon rice vinegar

Oil

8 Hawaiian rolls or any slider roll, toasted

1. Combine the green onion, bell pepper, ginger, and garlic in a food processor and pulse a couple of times.

2. Add the shrimp, panko, 3 tablespoons of the mayo, and the soy sauce and pulse until the shrimp are just coarsely chopped and combined—don't turn it into mush.

3. Form the shrimp mixture into eight small patties the size of your roll, set them on a tray lined with parchment or waxed paper, and chill them in the refrigerator for about an hour or so.

4. Combine the cabbage, remaining 3 tablespoons of mayo, sriracha, and rice vinegar in a medium bowl. Mix well and set aside.

5. Heat the oil in a large pan over medium-high heat, add the patties in a single layer, and cook for 4 to 5 minutes on each side until golden brown and gorgeous.

6. Build: put some slaw each bun bottom, and then set a patty on top and add the top bun.

ITALIAN SAUSAGE AND PEPPERS BURGER

Thick

I walk past ground Italian sausage all the time in the market, and one day finally realized I could make a burger out of it. And when I did, I was like, "What the hell just happened?" Get ready for the same reaction.

MAKES 2 BURGERS

¼ cup mayonnaise

3 large fresh basil leaves, chopped fine

1 big garlic clove, minced

Oil

½ red bell pepper, seeded and diced

½ yellow onion, diced

Kosher salt and freshly ground black pepper

5.3 ounces hot Italian sausage

5.3 ounces ground beef

2 slices provolone

2 ciabatta rolls

1. Combine the mayo, basil, and garlic in a small bowl, stir well, then set aside (and congratulations, you just made garlic-basil aioli and maybe didn't even know it!).

2. In a nonstick pan over medium-high heat, add a tablespoon of oil. Add the bell pepper and onion, season with a little salt and black pepper, and cook until well softened, 6 to 7 minutes. Remove from the heat and keep warm.

3. Combine the sausage and ground beef until just mixed, then form into two patties.

4. Add another tablespoon of oil to the pan, then add the patties and cook until done, adding the cheese when you flip.

5. Grill or toast the rolls and build: bun bottom, aioli, patty, bell pepper mixture, bun top.

HOISIN CHILI BURGER

Thick

Think of hoisin as Chinese barbecue sauce: thick, rich, and sweet, but with a different—though no less delicious—flavor profile. And in this case, hoisin, chili sauce, and sesame oil turn a regular burger into an "oh, holy crap" moment.

MAKES 2 BURGERS

10.6 ounces ground beef

2 garlic cloves, minced

2 teaspoons minced fresh ginger

4 green onions, white and light green parts, finely chopped

Kosher salt and freshly ground black pepper

2 tablespoons hoisin sauce

2 tablespoons Asian chili sauce

¾ cup broccoli coleslaw mix

2 tablespoons mayonnaise

½ teaspoon sesame oil

2 buns, grilled or toasted

1. Mix the ground beef with the garlic, ginger, green onion, salt, and pepper, then shape into two patties.

2. Combine the hoisin and chili sauce in a small bowl and set aside.

3. Mix together the broccoli slaw, mayo, and sesame oil in a separate bowl to create a slaw, then set aside.

4. Cook the burgers to your desired doneness, brushing each side with the hoisin sauce mixture, with a final brushing when the burgers come off the heat.

5. Serve the burgers in the buns with the slaw.

THE SAMBURGER

Smashed

Named after our burger restaurant and easily the best-selling burger on the menu. *Why?* you might ask. Because it's simplicity at its best: meat, cheese, onions, sauce, bun—it's just a damn fine combination. And I think this as a double is about as good as it gets, so don't hold back—just go for it. In fact, half a double is better than a whole single, for sure.

MAKES 1 DOUBLE BURGER

8 ounces ground beef (a blend here would be the best)

Oil

Kosher salt and freshly ground black pepper

2 slices American cheese

¼ cup Caramelized Onions (page 222)

2 buns (good ones like brioche)

¼ cup Burger Sauce (page 228)

1. Shape the beef into two balls and lightly oil a flat top, cast-iron pan, or griddle. Add the beef to the pan, smash down, and season with salt and pepper. Add the cheese to both when you flip.

2. Since this won't take long, it's the perfect time to reheat the onions, if necessary, and put the buns on the flat top to toast.

3. Build: bun bottom, sauce, patty, patty, onions, bun top.

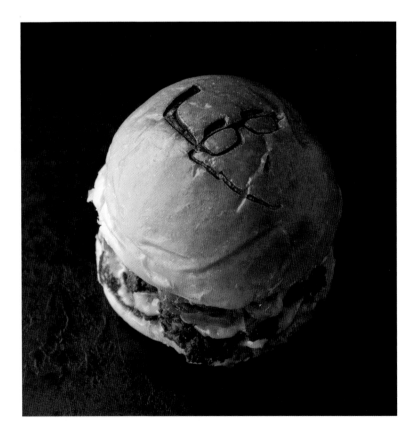

PEANUT BUTTER AND JELLY BURGER

Smashed

If Elvis could eat PB, banana, and bacon in a sandwich, we can eat PB&J on a burger. And the thing that makes this work for me is the combination of both sweet and savory. Oh, and the crispy fried onions don't hurt, either.

MAKES 2 BURGERS

8 ounces ground beef or chicken

Kosher salt and freshly ground black pepper

Oil

2 buns

¼ cup creamy peanut butter (actually, chunky is cool, too, though unnecessary because we have the crispy onions)

¼ cup jam (this is up to you, but I think raspberry or blackberry is a good call)

½ cup Crispy Onions (page 205)

1. Separate the beef into two balls.
2. Cook the patties until done, seasoning with salt and pepper as you put them on the oiled cooking surface.
3. Toast or grill the buns.
4. Build: bun bottom, peanut butter, patty, jam, onions, bun top.
5. Napkins.
6. Eat.

PASTRAMI BURGER

Smashed or Thick

Not "made of" pastrami (though, that wouldn't be bad at all); rather, made with pastrami "on it." There's just something about the fatty richness that made this an instant classic for *moi*.

MAKES 3 OR 4 BURGERS

1 pound ground beef

1½ teaspoons garlic powder

Kosher salt and freshly ground black pepper

2 tablespoons prepared yellow mustard

Swiss cheese slices

8 ounces thinly sliced deli pastrami

3 or 4 buns

Mayonnaise

1 dill pickle, cut into ⅛-inch disks

1. Put the ground beef in a bowl, add the garlic powder, salt, and pepper and mix to combine. Separate into three or four balls or patties.

2. Brush the tops of the patties with mustard, season with salt and pepper, and put on the grill mustard-side down to cook—brushing the now-exposed side of the patties with more mustard when you do.

3. When halfway done, flip the patties over and add the cheese.

4. Just as they're finishing, heat the pastrami in a nonstick pan over medium heat for about a minute a side—just until it starts glistening because you don't want it dry.

5. While they cook, toast the buns.

6. Build: bun bottom, mayo, pickles, patty, pastrami, bun top.

GARLIC BUTTER BURGER

Smashed or Thick

Okay, so call this what you will, but look at the picture and tell me it doesn't look insanely delicious. And of course it's not a burger made solely out of butter—it's a patty with garlic herb compound butter crammed in the middle. And whether you think it's right or wrong, you'll want it again.

MAKES 3 OR 4 BURGERS

4 tablespoons (½ stick) salted butter, at room temperature

2 large garlic cloves, finely minced

1 tablespoon finely chopped fresh herbs (parsley, cilantro, rosemary—use what you've got)

Kosher salt and freshly ground black pepper

⅓ cup mayonnaise

1 pound ground beef (beef is the way to go)

Sliced cheese (white Cheddar would be perfect)

Buns, toasted

Lettuce and tomato (generally not a fan of lettuce and tomato on a burger, but it works here)

1. Put the butter, half of the garlic, and the herbs, salt, and pepper in a small bowl. Mix really well to combine.

2. Transfer the mixture to the middle of a large piece of plastic wrap, roll into a tube, and twist the ends to make tight. Refrigerate until firm.

3. Mix the remaining garlic with the mayo in a small bowl and set aside.

4. Form the meat into two balls.

5. Remove the garlic butter from the fridge and unwrap. Cut two ¼-inch-thick disks. Gently press a disk into the middle of each ball, then gently form a patty around the disk.

6. Cook to your desired doneness, 3 to 4 minutes per side for medium rare. Add the cheese after you flip them.

7. Build: bun bottom, garlic mayo, lettuce, tomato, patty, bun top.

TURKEY BURGER (THAT DOESN'T SUCK)

Smashed or Thick

Okay, admittedly that was a bit mean to turkeys, but to be fair, I think we'd all agree that turkey can be a bit, oh, what's the word . . . boring. And so I present a not boring, not dry turkey burger that anyone can get behind, except for maybe the turkeys, of course.

MAKES 3 OR 4 BURGERS

1 tablespoon oil

1 red jalapeño pepper, seeded and sliced into thin strips

1 green jalapeño pepper, seeded and sliced into thin strips

½ yellow onion, sliced into thin strips

1 head Roasted Garlic (recipe follows)

⅓ cup + 2 tablespoons mayonnaise

Salt and freshly ground black pepper

1 pound ground turkey

2 tablespoons Dijon mustard

Muenster slices

1. Heat a skillet over medium heat and add the oil.
2. Add the jalapeños and onion and cook for about 20 minutes, or until lightly caramelized. Remove from the heat and set aside.
3. Combine the roasted garlic, ⅓ cup of the mayo, and a pinch each of salt and black pepper. Mix well, then set aside.
4. Put the ground turkey in a large bowl, add the Dijon mustard and remaining 2 tablespoons of mayo, and mix well.
5. Form the meat into three or four balls or patties and cook on a grill, seasoning with more salt and pepper once they hit the grill. Cook to an internal temp of between 155 and 160°F to keep them as juicy as possible.
6. Add the cheese when you flip.
7. Build: spread garlic mayo on the bun bottom (you won't use all of it), add the patty, caramelized pepper and onion, and the bun top.

ROASTED GARLIC

This is so different from fresh raw garlic because of its sweet, nutty flavor. It's perfect added to mayo, great with avocado toast—really great anywhere.

MAKE 1 HEAD

1 head garlic

Olive oil

1. Preheat your oven (or even toaster oven) to 400°F.
2. Cut ½ inch off the top of the head of garlic (the top is the pointy side).
3. Put the head, cut side up, on a sheet of foil and drizzle with about a teaspoon of olive oil. Wrap in the foil, sealing the edges well.
4. Bake for 40 minutes.
5. Remove from the oven and let cool enough so you can hold the head to remove the cloves—either using a paring knife to pull them out or squeezing them out of their skins with your fingers.
6. Use.

BUFFALO CHICKEN BURGER

Smashed or Thick

Not sure when this became a magical combination, but buffalo *anything* is pretty damn good. Make the sauce early (like a day or so before even) because it'll just get better, and you can use any leftovers for salad.

MAKES 3 OR 4 BURGERS

1 pound ground chicken

⅓ cup finely diced celery

⅓ cup finely diced green onion

¼ cup finely chopped fresh curly parsley

Kosher salt and freshly ground black pepper

⅓ cup Frank's RedHot Original Cayenne Pepper Sauce

⅓ cup panko bread crumbs

3 tablespoons mayonnaise

3 tablespoons sour cream

¼ cup blue cheese crumbles

1 garlic clove, minced

1 teaspoon Worcestershire sauce

3 or 4 buns (good ones like brioche)

Shredded lettuce

½ cup Crispy Onions (page 205)

1. Combine the chicken, celery, green onion, parsley, salt, pepper, 2 tablespoons of Frank's, and the panko bread crumbs in a medium bowl and mix well.

2. Form into three or four balls or patties, put on waxed or parchment paper, and refrigerate for least 30 minutes.

3. Meanwhile, combine the mayo, sour cream, blue cheese, garlic, and Worcestershire in a small bowl. Mix really well, breaking up the crumbles as you go, then set aside.

4. Cook the burgers, seasoning with salt and pepper when you put them on.

5. Once you flip the burgers over, brush the tops with more Frank's and cook them until done, brushing both sides when you take them off.

6. Grill or toast the buns.

7. Build: bun bottom, blue cheese sauce, lettuce, burger, crispy onions, bun top.

STUFFED BEER CAN BURGER

Thick, if that wasn't obvious

Pretty sure this was created with the aid of alcohol—and I don't mean in it—I mean in the people.

"Hey, Jessie, I got me an idea."

"What's that, Blade?"

"I say we take that beer can, shove it in a pile of beef, make a
    hole, then fill 'er up with mac and cheese, and cook it."

"We gonna drink the beer, Blade?

"It ain't about the beer, Jessie. It's about the burger."

"Then why we usin' the beer?"

"Oh, forget it. You're dumber'n a barrel of hair."

MAKES 3 BIG-ASS BURGERS

1½ pounds 80/20 ground beef

1 tablespoon + 1 teaspoon
    Montreal steak seasoning

1 teaspoon garlic powder

2 splashes of soy sauce

Kosher salt and freshly
    ground black pepper

Oil

One 12-ounce can of whatever—
    beer, soda, it doesn't matter—
    with the bottom outer half
    rinsed clean and dried

6 slices Monterey Jack

Mac and Cheese (recipe follows)

6 strips uncooked bacon

3 hamburger buns

Mayonnaise

1. Combine the ground beef, 1 tablespoon of the steak seasoning, garlic powder, soy sauce, salt, and pepper in a medium bowl.

2. Mix well, then roll into three equal-size balls. Transfer to a waxed paper– or parchment paper–lined baking sheet, separating them well.

3. Lightly oil the bottom half of the beer can, push it into a ball of beef (but not through the bottom), forming an indentation and bringing the ground beef about a third of the way up the side of the can. Slowly and carefully twist and/or pull out the can—you should have a nice deep indentation. Repeat with the two other balls.

4. Fold three of the cheese slices into quarters and place one folded slice at the bottom of each indentation. Fill up the indentation with the mac and cheese.

5. Starting at the bottom, wrap two pieces of bacon around the outside of each "burger."

6. Cover the mac and cheese with the remaining cheese slices and sprinkle a little bit of the remaing Montreal seasoning on top.

7. Cook the burgers indirect—which means not directly over the flame—until cooked through, probably 20 to 30 minutes.

8. When ready, toast or grill the buns, add some mayo to each bun bottom, set the burger on the mayo, and add the bun top.

MAC AND CHEESE

MAKES 3½ CUPS

2 cups dried elbow macaroni

1 tablespoon oil

1 cup diced onion

1 garlic clove, minced

¼ cup diced serrano pepper, about 6 peppers

¾ cup Cheez Whiz

1 teaspoon Montreal steak seasoning

1. Put the macaroni in a pot of boiling water, give it a quick stir, and cook for 7 to 8 minutes.

2. While it cooks, heat the oil in a skillet over medium-high heat, add the onion, and cook until just softened, about 3 minutes. Then add the garlic and serrano, cook for another minute, and remove from the heat.

3. Drain the mac when done, but hang onto about ½ cup of the cooking water.

4. Put the macaroni back into the pot. Add the Cheez Whiz, the onion mixture, and the steak seasoning. Mix well and remove from the heat.

5. Stir in a little bit of water at a time until it's to your preferred texture—I like it creamy—then set aside until it's time to use in the burgers.

THE OKLAHOMA BURGER

Smashed

I've never been to Oklahoma, but if the rest of their food is anything like this burger, I know I'd be happy there. Rumor has it that Oklahomans added onions to their burgers during the Great Depression to help stretch expensive hamburger meat. And whatever the reason, there's just a simple honestly to this burger that I love, right down to the "not even toasted or griddled bun."

MAKES 2 DOUBLE BURGERS

1 large white onion
1 pound ground beef (and it should be beef)
Oil
Kosher salt and freshly ground black pepper
2 slices American cheese
¼ cup mayonnaise
2 buns

1. Peel and slice the onion as absolutely thinly as you can—in fact, use a mandoline if you have one.

2. Gather up the slices and squeeze out as much liquid as you can, then set aside for now.

3. Separate the beef into four balls.

4. On a flat top over high heat, add a little oil, put on the balls, season with salt and pepper, and cover each with a pile of onion— you really shouldn't see any beef underneath at this point.

5. Smash down each heap of onion and beef to a thin patty, then cook for about a minute.

6. Flip, add the cheese, and finish cooking.

7. When ready, add some mayo to each bottom bun, then stack 2 patties with onions and cheese, then the bun top.

TRUFFLE PARTY SLIDERS

Extravagant? Actually, in taste only, because we aren't using actual truffles—we're using truffle cheese and truffle oil. But they'll definitely taste like a million bucks.

MAKES 12 SLIDERS

1 large yellow onion, diced

2 tablespoons oil

2 pounds ground beef

2 teaspoons kosher salt

2 teaspoons freshly
ground black pepper

2 teaspoons garlic powder

12 Hawaiian-style rolls (oh,
go on, just make them
real Hawaiian rolls)

½ cup mayonnaise

8 ounces truffle cheese, shredded

8 tablespoons (1 stick)
salted butter

2 garlic cloves, minced

2 tablespoons finely
chopped fresh parsley

2 teaspoons truffle oil

1. Preheat the oven to 350°F.

2. Cook the onion in 1 tablespoon of the oil in a large pan over medium heat until softened and beginning to caramelize, about 10 minutes, then remove from the heat and set aside.

3. Heat the remaining oil in the same pan, add the beef, season with the salt, pepper, and garlic powder, and cook, stirring to break up well, until cooked through.

4. Slice the rolls across the equator (in half horizontally) and put the bottoms in a 9-by-13-inch baking dish or separate them to fit into a round cast-iron pan (a Sam the Cooking Guy 12-inch cast-iron pan would do the job quite nicely, I might add).

5. No matter which pan is used, spread the rolls with the mayo and top with the cooked onion.

6. Add the beef, top with the shredded cheese, then put on the bun tops.

7. Melt the butter with the garlic, parsley, and truffle oil, mix well, and brush over the bun tops.

8. Bake, uncovered, for 15 to 20 minutes.

9. Separate into individual sliders and serve.

10. Oh my . . .

CHICKEN SMASH BURGER

Smashed, duh

When we made this for YouTube, I said, "This is not just one of the best chicken burgers I've ever had, it's one of the best burgers I've ever had—period," This burger is the reason we have chicken as an option at Samburgers, and I think many assume it'll be devoid of flavor, but *au contraire*, my friends—it's so good, it's wack.

MAKES 2 DOUBLE BURGERS

1 pound boneless chicken thighs—
   leave the fat on and follow
   the rules under "It's a Grind"
   (page 54) for how to grind them,
   or 1 pound ground chicken (but
   honestly, it won't be as good
   because it'll probably be ground
   breast or some weird bits)

1 serrano pepper, seeded if
   you don't want too much
   heat, diced small

1 teaspoon garlic powder

Kosher salt and freshly
   ground black pepper

Oil

½ red bell pepper, sliced
   into thin strips

½ small yellow onion, sliced thinly

4 slices Monterey Jack

Buns (something very decent),
   toasted or grilled

⅓ cup mayonnaise

¾ cup Crispy Onions (page 205)

1. Put the ground chicken into a bowl with the serrano, garlic powder, and ½ teaspoon each of salt and pepper. Mix well, then separate into four balls and refrigerate at least 30 minutes.

2. Heat a pan over medium-high heat, heat a tablespoon of oil, then add the bell pepper and onion. Let cook until beautifully softened, about 8 minutes, season to taste with salt and black pepper, then remove from the heat and set aside.

3. Cook the chicken, smashing it down, then season with salt and black pepper, about 2 minutes. Flip over, add a slice of cheese to each patty, and cook until done.

4. Build: bun bottom, mayo, two patties with cheese, some of the bell pepper mixture, crispy onions, and bun top.

5. Do I really need to suggest what comes next?

SANDWICHES

Look, I know bread slices are technically not really a bun—just as the tortillas in the taco or burrito chapters are not really buns. But *Sam the Cooking Guy: Between the Bread* as a title just didn't do anything for me. So sue me, it's my book.

But the inexactness of my title shouldn't keep you from loving this chapter because there's more history in this section than in any of the others. This is because the sandwich is presumed to have been the creation of John Montagu, the 4th Earl of Sandwich, way back in the 1700s. Apparently he was an avid card player, and in the middle of a game one evening, he requested meat placed between two slices of bread so he could eat without getting up from the table: eat with one hand and continue playing cards with the other. They say necessity is the mother of invention, and that night the hungry earl created culinary history.

Since that meager start, the sandwich has become universally loved and respected. But like the tacos, it doesn't matter what goes in between those slices of bread because it's still a sandwich.

FRENCH TOAST BREAKFAST SANDWICH

The only trick to this, and it's not much of a trick: to get the bread a little crispier than you usually would for French toast. After that, it's a breakfast dream come true.

MAKES 1 SANDWICH

3 large eggs

2 tablespoons milk

2 cups cornflakes

2 slices bread

3 tablespoons salted butter

2 slices brioche bread

1 slice Muenster

⅓ cup Caramelized Onions (page 222)

Kosher salt and freshly ground black pepper

2 hash browns, cooked and crispy

3 strips cooked bacon

Maple syrup (optional)

1. Beat two of the eggs and milk together in a wide, shallow bowl, then set aside.

2. Put the cornflakes in a large zippered bag, zip shut, and crush well. Transfer to a plate and set aside.

3. Dip the bread first into the egg, and then into the cornflakes, pushing down on both sides to make sure the crushed flakes stick well.

4. Heat a large skillet over medium heat and add 2 tablespoons of the butter. When the butter is melted, add the battered bread to the pan.

5. Cook until both slices are golden and crispy, then flip over, adding the cheese to one of the pieces. Continue to cook until golden on the bottom.

6. In a separate pan, melt the last tablespoon of butter and fry the remaining egg with a little salt and pepper, keeping the yolk intact and runny.

7. Build: base piece of French toast with cheese, caramelized onions, hash browns, bacon, egg, and top piece of French toast. Serve with maple syrup for dunking or drizzling—or both.

CHORIZO AND GUACAMOLE TORTA

We went to Mexico a bunch of years ago, and the last thing I ate before we came back was this. And the first thing I made when we got back was this. If you can find a torta roll to use, all the better. If you can't find one it's not a huge deal; just use something a little crispy on the outside, like a small baguette.

MAKES 2 SANDWICHES

10 ounces Mexican chorizo—pork, beef, and even soy chorizo work great

⅓ cup diced yellow onion

2 torta rolls

1 cup shredded iceberg lettuce

1 cup shredded Monterey Jack

⅔ cup Guacamole (page 230)

1. Heat the broiler.

2. Cook the chorizo and onion together in a pan over medium heat until the chorizo is done, 7 to 8 minutes.

3. Slice the rolls in half horizontally and lightly toast, cut side up, under the broiler.

4. Remove from the broiler and build: bun bottom, lettuce, chorizo, cheese—then put back under the broiler just until the cheese melts. Take out and add guacamole and then the bun top.

5. Love it.

GRILLED PB&J SANDWICH

Best recipe in the book? Maybe. Dumbest recipe in the book? Most definitely.

MAKES 1 SANDWICH

Bread of choice

Peanut butter of choice
(smooth, crunchy, etc.)

Jelly, any flavor (though
I'd reach for raspberry
before anything else)

Salted butter

Potato chips

1. Heat a nonstick pan over medium heat.

2. Cover one slice of bread with peanut butter and the other with the jelly—by the way, you saw this coming, right?

3. Put the two halves together, butter both outer sides of the sando, and then place in the preheated pan.

4. Now cook just like a grilled cheese until both sides are golden brown.

5. Remove, open up, add the chips, close up, and eat.

Sweet, savory, salty, crispy, smooth, and warm—what more could you possibly need?

GRILLED CHICKEN EGG SALAD SANDWICH

I saw a chicken salad recipe once that, in addition to the chicken, also had grapes, raisins, and cranberries. Just let that sink in, because that was no chicken salad. It might have been a fruit salad, but almost nothing more, and I'm still mad about it. But I hope you know I'd never do that to you, ever. This recipe is one delicious chicken salad . . . no fruit.

MAKES 2 SANDWICHES

3 to 4 small chicken thighs, or about 1½ cups shredded or diced cooked chicken

Kosher salt and freshly ground black pepper to taste

2 hard-boiled eggs, peeled, then grated or chopped small

3 tablespoons red bell pepper, seeded and diced small

3 tablespoons mayonnaise— or more or less, depending on how you like it (mayo is a deeply personal thing)

½ celery stalk, diced small to get about ¼ cup

2 teaspoons curry powder

1 tablespoon finely chopped fresh parsley

1 tablespoon finely chopped green onion

A few pieces of romaine lettuce (people often use a leafy green like butter lettuce, but that's too wimpy and weak— romaine will stand up)

4 slices bread of choice (literally any will be great)

1. If cooking the chicken, season it with salt and pepper and grill until done—let cool and dice.

2. Put the cooked chicken in a bowl with all the remaining ingredients, except the bread and romaine, and mix well to combine.

3. Make it into a sandwich with the romaine beneath the chicken.

CHICKEN KATSU SANDO

Japanese chicken katsu is one of my all-time faves: crispy panko-crusted chicken sliced into strips and served on rice with a ridiculously flavorful katsu sauce—think tangy steak sauce. And in a sandwich, it's way different but still great because of the crispiness of the chicken inside the supersoft white bread. Oh, and by the way, we're cheating a bit by using Western steak sauce and not having to run around to find actual katsu sauce.

MAKES 1 SANDWICH

1 small boneless, skinless
    chicken breast

Kosher salt and freshly
    ground black pepper

1 cup all-purpose flour

1 large egg, beaten

1 cup panko bread crumbs

Oil

2 tablespoons steak sauce

2 tablespoons mayonnaise

1 teaspoon Worcestershire sauce

2 slices white bread (don't
    hate me, just trust me)

½ cup (loosely filled)
    shredded green cabbage

1. Put the chicken breast in a large zippered bag, zip shut, and flatten evenly to about ½ inch thick. Remove from the bag and season with salt and pepper.

2. Put the flour, egg, and panko into three separate wide bowls, then coat the chicken first in the flour—shaking off the excess—then into the egg, and finally in the panko, being sure to coat it well.

3. Heat about ½ inch of oil in a medium pan to 350°F and carefully add the chicken.

4. Cook for 3 to 4 minutes on each side, until the internal temp reaches about 165°F and it's beautifully golden brown. Transfer to a paper towel to drain.

5. While it cooks, combine the steak sauce, mayo, and Worcestershire in a small bowl and set aside.

6. Build: one bread slice, steak sauce mayo, cabbage, chicken, a little more of the steak sauce mayo, and then the second bread slice.

7. Cut off all four edges, then cut the sandwich into three sections.

TOMATO AND POTATO CHIP SANDWICH

It's 1979, I'm living in my first apartment on South Marine Drive in Vancouver ($235 a month, by the way), and my upstairs neighbor is Kevin McDermid, a good friend and a really great kid fresh off the boat from Scotland (it was actually a plane, but the boat expression is way better). He taught me all kinds of things about Scotland, not the least of which was this simple yet amazing sandwich. Please don't mess with it—just make it exactly as is.

MAKES 2 SANDWICHES

¼ cup Heinz salad cream (a tangy mayo-ish thing if you can find it; if not, any of these will do: Kewpie or Duke's mayonnaise, or Miracle Whip)

4 slices soft white bread

1 small, perfectly ripe tomato, sliced into ⅛-inch slices

Kosher salt and freshly ground black pepper

2 small handfuls plain potato chips

1. Spread the salad cream on all slices of the bread.

2. Add an even layer of the tomato on one slice.

3. Season with salt and pepper.

4. Add the chips, then the second slice of bread, salad cream side down.

5. Use your hand to squish flat, then cut in half diagonally.

6. Eat.

ROAST BEEF DIP WITH ONION GRAVY

Yes, this is maybe more than you bargained for, and you could always use a good roast beef from the deli. But I'm giving you my mom's really solid roast beef recipe, and some would see it as a little disrespectful not to use it. Sooo . . .

MAKES MANY SANDWICHES

One 4- to 5-pound roast beef (you can't make a roast for a single sandwich, so appreciate you're just going to have extra and be happy about it)

Kosher salt and freshly ground black pepper

5 garlic cloves, minced, plus 1 more, minced, to use later

¼ cup prepared yellow mustard

1 tablespoon oil

½ cup diced yellow onion

2 tablespoons vermouth or white wine

2 cups beef stock

2 tablespoons cold water

1 tablespoon cornstarch

2 slices sturdy bread, such as sourdough

2 slices Muenster

2 tablespoons prepared horseradish sauce

1. Take the roast out of the fridge about 2 hours before cooking and pat dry with paper towels.

2. Preheat the oven to 450°F.

3. Season generously with salt and pepper.

4. Combine the 5 minced garlic cloves and mustard in a small bowl, mix well, and rub over the entire roast.

5. Put the roast in a baking dish or on a rack on a baking sheet, and then into the oven for 20 minutes. Lower the heat to 325°F and cook for 12 to 15 minutes per pound until you get the temp you want. For medium rare, look for an instant-read thermometer to read 125°F in the center of the roast, or about 130°F for medium.

6. Once you hit your temp, take the roast out of the oven and allow it to rest for 20 to 30 minutes before carving—it will rise an additional 5°F while it rests. After it's rested, you're ready to carve—but for the sando, maybe let it cool down even more.

7. While the roast cooks, heat the oil in small pot and add the onion and remaining minced garlic. Stir well and allow to begin to soften, which will take a couple of minutes.

8. Add the vermouth, stirring well, and, after about a minute, put in the beef stock and season with a little salt and pepper.

9. Stir and let simmer for about 20 minutes.

10. Mix together the cold water and cornstarch in a small bowl until blended.

11. Add the cornstarch mixture to the stock mixture, give it a stir, and let simmer—it will start to thicken. When the gravy is at the consistency you want—I like it thick enough to coat the back of a spoon—remove from the heat and set aside.

12. Toast the bread lightly, and while it toasts, thinly slice about 5 ounces of the cooked roast for each sandwich. In a nonstick pan with a lid (you'll need that later) over medium heat, add your pile of sliced roast beef.

13. Heat until warm on one side, then flip over and add the cheese; put a lid on the pan to help it melt.

14. Build: spread the horseradish on one side of the bread, add the pile of cheesy roast beef, then the other slice of bread.

15. Warm up the gravy and put in a small bowl to dip the sandwich into.

CHICKEN BACON RANCH SANDWICH

The thing that really makes this are the fresh herbs. And in an early version of this recipe, I'd included their dried equivalents but then decided against it. Because made with only dried, it wouldn't even be close.

MAKES 3 OR 4 SANDWICHES

¼ cup mayonnaise

¼ cup sour cream

¼ cup buttermilk or milk

2 tablespoons chopped fresh parsley

2 tablespoons chopped fresh dill

2 tablespoons chopped fresh chives or green onions

2 garlic cloves, finely minced

½ teaspoon onion powder

¼ teaspoon kosher salt

½ teaspoon freshly ground black pepper

Juice of ½ lemon

Oil

2 boneless, skinless chicken breasts

Blackening Seasoning (recipe follows)

3 tablespoons salted butter

6 or 9 slices bread

Shredded iceberg lettuce

6 to 8 strips cooked, crispy bacon

1. Prepare the ranch: combine the mayo, sour cream, buttermilk, parsley, dill, chives, half of the garlic, and the onion powder, salt, pepper, and lemon juice in a large bowl. Mix well, then refrigerate—you can easily do this a day or two before because it'll get better with time.

2. When ready to cook the chicken, heat a pan over high heat to almost smoking—cast iron would be an excellent choice here.

3. Lightly oil the chicken and season liberally with the blackening seasoning.

4. Turn on your fan (if cooking inside) and cook the chicken in the pan, turning often, until it hits an internal temp of 160°F. Remove from the pan, let cool, then cut into a medium dice.

5. Put the diced chicken into a bowl, add about half of the mayo/herb combo, and mix well to combine. You can add more mayo/herb combo, if that's your preference.

6. Melt the butter with the remaining minced garlic, brush it on one side of all the bread slices, then grill, butter side down, on a flat top or nonstick pan until toasty.

7. Build: bread with the grilled side down, top with extra ranch, lettuce, the chicken, bacon, and the top piece of bread.

BLACKENING SEASONING

MAKES ABOUT ½ CUP

3 tablespoons smoked paprika

2 teaspoons onion powder

1½ teaspoons sea salt

1 teaspoon garlic powder

1 teaspoon freshly ground black pepper

1 teaspoon dried thyme

1 teaspoon dried oregano

1 teaspoon cayenne pepper

Combine everything in a small bowl and mix well. Store in an airtight container.

HOT ITALIAN SANDWICH

This is sandwich simplicity at its best. It's delicious for a start, but it's also warm, spicy, melty, and crispy—which makes it perfect.

MAKES 1 SANDWICH

Italian roll, small baguette, ciabatta, focaccia—any will be awesome

⅓ cup mixed Italian hot peppers, such as giardiniera (recipe follows, or use store-bought)

9 to 12 slices (depending on the size of roll) mixed Italian sandwich meats: prosciutto, capocollo, soppressata, prosciutto, etc.

2 tablespoons Garlic Aioli (page 229)

3 or 4 slices fresh mozzarella, about ⅛ inch thick

1. Preheat the oven to 325°F.
2. Slice the roll lengthwise, but not all the way through—leave a hinge.
3. Spread aioli on the bottom half, add the giardiniera, and top with the meats; put mozzarella on the top half.
4. Place the sandwich, open faced, on a baking sheet, then bake until the cheese is melted and the bread is crisp and toasty, 10 to 15 minutes.
5. Fold together, slice in half, and eat.

GIARDINIERA

MAKES ABOUT 2 CUPS

½ head small cauliflower, chopped pretty small

3 celery stalks, diced small

2 medium carrots, diced small

1 red bell pepper, seeded and diced small

2 serrano peppers, seeded and finely diced

2 jalapeño peppers, seeded and finely diced

¼ cup salt

2 garlic cloves, minced

½ cup white wine vinegar

1 teaspoon dried oregano

½ cup olive oil

Kosher salt

1. Put the cauliflower, celery, carrots, peppers, and salt in a medium bowl. Mix well, cover with cold water, and refrigerate, covered, overnight—about 12 hours.
2. Drain and rinse the vegetables.
3. Combine the garlic, vinegar, oregano, and oil in a large bowl, mix well, and then add the drained vegetables.
4. Add salt to taste, toss to mix, and refrigerate, covered.
5. You can use it on the same day, but it'll be better the next day.
6. Transfer to jars, cover, and refrigerate for up to 3 weeks.

PHILLY CHEESESTEAK

The times I've eaten this out someplace and it sucked, it sucked because they either used a shitty or wrong cut of beef and/or the onion and peppers weren't caramelized enough. That's it, nothing else. It's honestly not complicated. A mediocre bun can be dealt with. Even wrong cheese will work. I mean with provolone and Cheez Whiz as the main contenders—pretty much anything in between is fair game.

So, trust me on this one: buy a rib eye even if you don't like a rib eye. Because in addition to just being better, it's definitely more forgiving and harder to mess up. And let your veggies cook long enough to get gorgeous and caramelized.

MAKES 3 SANDWICHES

Oil

1 green bell pepper, sliced thinly

1 small yellow onion, sliced thinly

1 pound rib-eye steak, thinly sliced (freezing it for about 45 minutes first will make it way easier to cut thinly . . . and trust me, too thin is not a problem)

Kosher salt and freshly ground black pepper

2 tablespoons Worcestershire sauce

4 slices provolone or ⅔ cup Cheez Whiz

3 fresh sandwich buns, sliced in half crosswise and lightly toasted

1. Heat the oil in a large skillet (if using provolone, make sure your pan has a lid) over medium-high heat and cook the bell pepper and onion until deepening in color and beautifully softened, maybe 15 minutes.

2. Season the meat with salt and pepper.

3. Increase the heat to high, push the veggies to one side, add a little more oil, then add the meat and cook until almost no longer pink.

4. Mix the onion mixture into the meat, add the Worcestershire, stir, and then form into two piles the size of the buns.

5. If using provolone, add it now to the top of the meat mixture and cover the skillet. Allow to melt, then transfer to the bun bottom, add the bun top, and eat.

6. If using Cheez Whiz, put it in a small microwave-safe bowl and microwave until melty and slowly pourable.

7. Add the meat mixture to the bun bottom, pour on some cheese, add the bun top, and eat.

BANH MI

The veggies make this—all the veggies. The pickled stuff gives it a nice vinegar punch; the jalapeños, some heat; and of course, the cilantro adds beautiful freshness.

MAKES 3 SANDWICHES

1 pork tenderloin (about 1 pound)
Marinade (recipe follows)
⅓ cup mayonnaise
2 tablespoons sriracha
1 traditional baguette, sliced in half lengthwise, leaving a hinge, then cut into thirds across
1 Persian cucumber, sliced thinly
Pickled Daikon and Carrot (recipe follows)
1 red jalapeño pepper, sliced thinly
1 green jalapeño pepper, sliced thinly
1 bunch fresh cilantro for garnish

1. Put the pork tenderloin in a zippered plastic bag, add the marinade, seal it, then mix it all around to cover. Refrigerate for 3 hours.

2. On a grill over medium-high heat, remove the tenderloin from the bag (reserving marinade), and grill until cooked evenly all the way through, about 3 minutes each side (assuming there are sort of four sides), flipping often, until its internal temp reaches 145°F.

3. While it cooks, pour the reserved marinade into a small pot and bring to a boil over medium-high heat. Let boil for a couple of minutes until reduced by about half, then remove from the heat and set aside to cool.

4. Thinly slice the tenderloin against the grain.

5. Spread the mayo, sriracha, plus some of the reduced marinade on the bottom portions of the baguette. Add the tenderloin, cucumber, pickled daikon and carrot, jalapeños, and garnish with fresh cilantro.

MARINADE

MAKES ABOUT 1 CUP

½ cup soy sauce
3 tablespoons sugar
3 tablespoons Asian fish sauce
2 garlic cloves, pressed
1 tablespoon sriracha
Juice of 1 lime

Mix together all the marinade ingredients in a small bowl.

PICKLED DAIKON AND CARROT

MAKES ABOUT 1 CUP

½ cup daikon radish matchsticks
½ carrot, cut into matchsticks
½ cup rice vinegar
1 teaspoon sugar
½ teaspoon salt

Mix together the radish, carrot, rice vinegar, sugar, and salt in a small bowl. Cover and place in the refrigerator until needed.

BACON, LETTUCE, FRIED TOMATO—BLFT

Your basic BLT is one of the cornerstones of sandwich life. Now, add fried crispy tomato and sweet spicy bacon, and you've created an effing legend.

MAKES 2 SANDWICHES

5 tablespoons maple syrup

1 tablespoon light brown sugar

½ teaspoon chipotle chile powder

1½ teaspoons Dijon mustard

8 strips uncooked bacon

2 cups all-purpose flour

2 large eggs, beaten

2 cups cornmeal

Kosher salt and freshly
   ground black pepper

1 large red tomato, not
   overly ripe, sliced into four
   ¼-inch-thick slices

Oil for frying

2 tablespoons Western-
   style chili sauce

2 tablespoons mayonnaise

4 slices bread

Iceberg lettuce

1. Preheat the oven to 400°F.

2. Combine 3 tablespoons of the maple syrup, the brown sugar, chipotle chile powder, and mustard in a small bowl and mix well to form a glaze.

3. Arrange the bacon in a single layer on a rack on a baking sheet, brush both sides with the glaze, and bake until it reaches your preferred crispiness—for me, this is between 30 and 40 minutes.

4. While the bacon bakes, put the flour on one plate, the beaten eggs in a wide bowl, and the cornmeal on another plate, seasoning the cornmeal with salt and pepper. Dip both sides of the tomato slices into the flour, then the beaten egg, and finally coat them in the cornmeal.

5. Heat about ½ inch of oil in a medium skillet over medium-high heat until 350°F, then fry the tomatoes until golden, 3 minutes per side.

6. Mix the chili sauce and mayo together in a bowl and set aside.

7. Toast or grill the bread, then build: slice of bread, mayo mixture, lettuce, bacon, fried tomatoes, and a second slice of bread spread with the mayo mixture.

BACON, EGG, AND CHEESE—BEC

The BEC is a classic New York breakfast sandwich, often grabbed on the way to work from a street cart or a deli.

MAKES 1 SANDWICH

3 strips uncooked bacon

1 teaspoon salted butter

2 large eggs, lightly beaten

Kosher salt and freshly ground black pepper

Kaiser roll

2 tablespoons mayonnaise

1 slice cheese (American is the way to go, but any good melting cheese would be okay—just don't tell anyone in New York)

1 teaspoon sriracha (in NY, it's often ketchup and I'm not a fan, plus I love this for a little touch of heat)

1. Cook the bacon until done your way; for me, that's part crispy and part still soft/fatty.

2. Heat a skillet over medium heat, add the butter, and when melted, pour in the eggs—I like to let them settle into a wide circle—then season lightly with salt and pepper.

3. Slice the roll in half horizontally and grill or toast until golden.

4. When the bottom of the eggs are about halfway set, add the cheese to the middle, then fold over until the approximate shape of the roll.

5. Spread half the mayo and sriracha on the bun bottom, add the eggs and bacon, spread the remaining mayo on the bun top, and close up.

6. Yum.

GRILLED HAM AND CHEESE SANDWICH

If a simple grilled cheese is wonderful, and a grilled ham and cheese is wonderfuller, that makes this one with caramelized onions and Black Forest ham the absolute wonderfullest!

MAKE 2 SANDWICHES

Dijon mustard

Mayonnaise

4 slices hearty bread (sourdough, Italian, pugliese—just nothing light and wimpy)

8 slices Lacey Swiss cheese (softer and a bit milder than regular Swiss)

8 slices Black Forest ham

⅔ cup Caramelized Onions (page 222)

Salted butter

1. Spread mustard and mayo on two slices of the bread, then to each of those add half the cheese, half the ham, half the caramelized onions, the remaining cheese, and another slice of bread.

2. Heat a nonstick pan over medium heat.

3. Spread butter on the top of each sandwich, and place, butter side down, in the heated pan.

4. Cook until golden brown, add butter to the top side, then turn over and cook until also golden.

5. Remove from the heat, cut in half, and eat.

GARLIC BREAD STEAK SANDWICH

My youngest, Zach, suggested a garlic bread grilled cheese, and somehow I went this direction with it. In any case, this was the thing that really started an increase in our YouTube subscribers, and for good reason—it's effing ridiculous. And by the way, Zach is a very talented commercial Realtor, who you should definitely call for all your commercial property needs. You can reach him at 858-822-XXXX. Hahaha, I really wanted to, but probably a bad idea.

MAKES 2 SANDWICHES

One 1-pound rib-eye steak

Oil

Kosher salt and freshly ground black pepper

¼ cup mayonnaise

1 tablespoon sriracha

1½ teaspoons Worcestershire sauce

4 tablespoons (½ stick) salted butter, at room temperature

1 large garlic clove, minced

2 tablespoons finely chopped fresh parsley

4 slices bread (go with something hearty—this is a big, meaty sando that requires something with fortitude)

1 cup baby arugula

½ cup Caramelized Onions (page 222)

1. Remove the steak from the refrigerator 30 minutes before cooking.

2. Heat a grill, grill pan, or even a cast-iron pan to medium-high heat, lightly oil the steak, season it well with salt and pepper, and put it on the grill.

3. Cook until medium rare (please) by turning the steak a lot every couple of minutes—this will keep it from getting that unwanted gray ring and will end up a beautiful medium rare throughout. To get there, use a digital instant-read thermometer starting about 10 minutes in and remove it when it hits approximately 130°F. Let the steak rest for 15 minutes.

4. Combine the mayo, sriracha, and Worcestershire in a small bowl, then set aside.

5. Mix the butter with the garlic, parsley, and a pinch of salt in a separate small bowl and brush on one side of each piece of bread.

6. Combine the arugula, ½ teaspoon of oil, and a pinch of salt and pepper in a medium bowl and mix well.

7. Slice the steak nice and thin across the grain.

8. In a nonstick pan over medium heat, put in the slices of bread, butter side down, and cook until beautifully golden on the buttered side. Then flip over and give the unbuttered side a little love for some color and crispness.

9. Remove from the pan, add the mayo sauce to two of the toasted bread slices (buttered side down), then layer on the arugula, steak, onions, and finally the remaining slices of bread.

MY MOM'S FAVOURITE SHRIMP SALAD SANDWICH

My mom and I used to argue "who makes it better" over a lot of foods. Steaks, sandwiches, even chopped liver—by the way, my chopped liver kills hers, and I mean that in the nicest, most loving way possible (the recipe is on my website). This is my version of one of her faves that, as she got older (the 'ol girl made it to an impressive 96 years, btw), she stopped making but would still get from a small golf course coffee shop near her house. It's just a great sandwich with wonderful memories. And I spelled it "favourite" the way she would spell it in Canada.

MAKES 2 SANDWICHES

1 teaspoon kosher salt, plus more for seasoning

1 lemon, cut into quarters

10 ounces raw 31/40 shrimp, "p-and-d" as they say (peeled and deveined)

¼ cup mayonnaise

2 tablespoons Western-style chili sauce (not the Asian kind)

2 teaspoons sriracha

¼ cup finely diced celery

2 tablespoons finely chopped fresh parsley

Freshly ground black pepper

2 brioche buns

¾ cup shredded iceberg lettuce

1. Bring a medium pot of water to a simmer, add the salt, and squeeze in the juice of two of the lemon quarters (then toss in the squeezed quarters, too).

2. When the salt has dissolved, add the shrimp and cook just until pink, about 2 minutes.

3. Transfer the shrimp to an ice-filled bowl to stop the cooking, then drain on paper towels. Discard the simmered lemon quarters.

4. Cut the shrimp into smallish bite-size pieces and put in a bowl with the mayo, chili sauce, sriracha, celery, parsley, and a teaspoon of juice from the remaining lemon quarters.

5. Season with salt and pepper and mix well.

6. Toast the buns, add some of the lettuce and the shrimp salad to each bun bottom, and finish with its bun top.

CHORI-POLLO SANDWICH

The inspiration for this comes from my friend Greg in Cleveland, who gets it from his favorite Mexican restaurant, but as a plate—not a sandwich. When he first told me about it, I laughed, saying no self-respecting Mexican restaurant in San Diego would ever name anything something stupid like that (it means "chorizo and chicken"), but after abusing him endlessly, I thought I'd be fair and try it—I am a reasonable man after all. Let's just say that even though I think the name is still dopey, the combination is so good we now have a version of it as a flatbread at our restaurant Graze, and obviously here as a sandwich.

MAKES 4 SANDWICHES

Oil

4 boneless, skinless chicken thighs

Kosher salt and freshly ground black pepper

12 ounces beef, pork, or soy chorizo (they're all good)

4 ounces canned diced green chiles

½ teaspoon ground cumin

Juice of 1 lime

1 small bunch cilantro, tops only

4 rolls (ciabatta would be sweet here, not sugar sweet but good sweet . . . you know what I mean)

½ cup Garlic Aioli (page 229)

1 cup shredded mozzarella or Monterey Jack

1. Lightly oil the chicken, season with salt and pepper, and grill, broil, or panfry until done—whatever works for you—then remove from the heat and let cool.

2. Meanwhile, cook the chorizo in a small pan until cooked through, and set aside.

3. Combine the chiles, cumin, lime juice, and cilantro in a blender or processor and whiz until blended.

4. Preheat the broiler.

5. Cut the chicken into smallish, bite-size pieces, place in a bowl, add the chile mixture, and toss to combine.

6. Slice the rolls, buns, whatever horizontally and put under the broiler until just getting a little color, then remove from the heat.

7. Add garlic aioli to the bottom of each roll, then some chorizo, then the chicken, and finally some cheese.

8. Put back under the broiler just until the cheese is melted, then remove from the heat, top with the upper half of each roll, and away you go.

GRILLED CUBANO

A recent trip to Miami reminded me how great this combo is. I mean, the insides are stupendous, but then the grilling to get it über-crispy all over is fantastic. Don't wanna make your own pork? I suppose you could always buy it, but . . .

MAKES 4 SANDWICHES

1 pork tenderloin (about 1 pound)

Kosher salt and freshly ground black pepper

½ teaspoon garlic powder

⅓ cup prepared yellow mustard

Mojo Sauce (recipe follows)

4 Cuban, Italian, or hoagie-type rolls

16 slices Swiss cheese

2 large dill pickles, sliced thinly lengthwise

½ pound thinly sliced Black Forest ham

8 tablespoons (1 stick) salted butter

1. Heat a grill to medium-high.

2. Season the pork with salt, pepper, and the garlic powder.

3. Rub about a tablespoon of the mustard on the pork (reserving the rest) and grill, turning often (brushing with some of the mojo as you go), until you have nice grill marks and the internal temp of the pork is between 140 and 145°F. Remove from the grill, let rest for 20 minutes, and lower the heat of the grill to medium.

4. Slice the buns horizontally, drizzle some of the mojo sauce on each cut side, and put facedown on the grill. Let them start to get a bit toasty, then remove from the grill.

5. Build for each: add a layer of the mustard to one of the grilled sides, two slices of the cheese, a layer of pickles, some of the ham, the pork, two more slices of cheese, and finally the other half of the mojo-grilled bun.

6. Butter the top of each sandwich and place each entire sandwich, butter side down, on the grill, weighted down with a cast-iron pan, a few lighter pans, a brick, or whatever you've got. Alternatively, you could always butter both sides of the sando and grill in a panini press contraption.

7. When you have nice grill marks, remove the weight, butter what is now the top, flip over, and repeat.

8. Pull off the grill when it's toasty, beautifully marked, and the cheese is melty.

MOJO SAUCE

MAKES ABOUT ⅓ CUP

3 garlic cloves, mashed smooth

¼ cup fresh orange juice

Juice of 1 lime

¼ teaspoon dried oregano

¼ teaspoon ground cumin

Pinch each of kosher salt and freshly ground black pepper

2 tablespoons oil

Put all the ingredients in a small bowl or squeeze bottle, then mix or shake well to combine. Set aside until needed.

CHOPPED CHEESE SANDWICH

Welcome back to *"Hey, I'm cookin' here"* New York. Bodegas are small markets that are dotted all over the city, and this classic bodega fave is fun to make. And I say that because you essentially cook the ground beef like a patty, but when it's just done, you chop it up—which seems silly, but it's not. You get all that great beefy crust, but in sort of a loose ground beef format. It's pretty genius. Oh, and ketchup again is typically used, but I swap it for Western-style chili sauce, which I think makes it way more interesting.

MAKES 1 SANDWICH

8 ounces ground beef

Kosher salt and freshly ground black pepper

Oil

½ small yellow onion, sliced

3 slices American cheese

1 soft, hoagie-type roll

¼ cup mayonnaise

2 tablespoons Western-style chili sauce

½ cup shredded iceberg lettuce

3 tomato slices

1. Form the beef into two patties, season with salt and pepper, and put on a lightly oiled flat top. Beside them, also put on the sliced onion.

2. Cook until there's a really nice sear on the bottom of the patties, then flip over. While they cook, stir the onion a bit; you want it to get an even color.

3. When the patties are nearly cooked through and beautifully seared on both sides, use two spatulas to start chopping them up.

4. As you do, add the onion to the beef and chop the patties and onion together.

5. Form the meat into the size of your bread and add the cheese; let it melt.

6. Slice the roll horizontally, leaving a hinge, and grill on the flat top to get some color and crisping.

7. Build: on both inner sides of the bread, spread the mayo and chili sauce, and then down the middle add the cheesy beef, lettuce, tomato, and finally a pinch each of salt and pepper.

8. Fold up (if you can) and eat.

TERIYAKI SPAM SLIDERS

According to the Internet, on average residents of Guam consume 16 cans of Spam per person per year. Next is Hawaii, at seven cans per person per year—and in either place that's a lot of Spam. I think it's like cilantro, in that you love or hate it—and I love it. Because when you grill or fry it in a pan, it gets all crispy and superdelicious. So, don't be a snob, and give this a go . . .

MAKES 6 SLIDERS

½ large onion, sliced thinly

Oil

One 12-ounce can Spam, sliced horizontally into 6 even pieces

6 Hawaiian roll-size pineapple slices, ¼ inch thick

⅓ cup teriyaki sauce (a thick one if you can find it)

3 tablespoons mayonnaise, Kewpie Japanese mayonnaise would be perfect for these

6 Hawaiian rolls, cut in half and lightly toasted

1. Cook the onion in a little oil on a flat top or large pan over medium heat until beautifully softened, about 5 minutes, then push to the side.

2. Add a little more oil and put on the Spam and pineapple—cook until both are nicely browned on the bottom.

3. Mix half of the teriyaki sauce with all of the mayo in a small bowl and set aside.

4. Flip the Spam and pineapple over and brush with some of the remaining teriyaki sauce.

5. When the bottoms of the Spam and pineapple are lightly browned, flip again and brush on more teriyaki sauce.

6. Build: put some of the mayo mixture on the bottom of each bun, add some onion, the Spam, the pineapple, and finally the bun top.

FRIED BALONEY AND CHEESE SANDWICH

Perhaps this and the Spam should have been in their own "strange meat" section. Wherever they belong—they definitely belong because plenty of the world eats this stuff and this is one of my favorite quick sandwiches. Oh sure, it's an effing five-napkin-mess to eat, but it's wonderful. And I know the proper spelling is *bologna*, but that's ridiculous and I refuse to write it like that.

MAKES 1 SANDWICH

1 teaspoon oil

½ medium yellow onion, sliced thinly

4 slices baloney

2 slices American cheese

1 hamburger-style bun

1 tablespoon grainy mustard

1 tablespoon mayonnaise

2 large tomato slices

1. Heat the oil in a small skillet over medium heat, add the onion, and cook for about 5 minutes, or until softened.

2. Evenly space out three ⅛-inch cuts around the outside edge of the baloney to prevent it from curling up, then place on a heated flat griddle or nonstick pan over medium heat.

3. Cook for 2 to 3 minutes on each side until the edges become a bit golden. Make two stacks of two baloney slices each, then add the cheese to the top of each stack and let melt.

4. Lightly toast the cut sides of the bun and build: spread mustard and mayo on the bun bottom, the onion, the tomato, then the two stacks of baloney and the bun top.

LOBSTER ROLL

At the risk of pissing off the Eastern Seaboard of the United States, let me say I think most of its lobster rolls are . . . well, a little same same, meaning kinda boring. Lobster: good. Lobster with butter: even better. But lobster rolls *can* be more. And we do that by adding just a couple of extra things for flavor and something great for texture—panko. So, sit back and get ready to tell your back-East friends there's a new lobster roll in town.

MAKES 2 ROLLS

Two 4- to 5-ounce lobster tails

8 tablespoons (1 stick) salted butter

2 garlic cloves, minced

¼ teaspoon smoked paprika

Zest and juice of ½ lemon

Pinch each of kosher salt and freshly ground black pepper

2 tablespoons panko bread crumbs

3 tablespoons diced celery

1 tablespoon finely chopped celery leaves or fresh curly parsley

1 tablespoon chopped fresh dill

2 tablespoons mayonnaise

2 top-split lobster or brioche buns, grilled to golden brown

1. Steam the lobster tail or drop it in simmering water. In either case, remove them after 4 minutes, assuming they're now opaque, then let cool slightly.

2. Put all but 1 tablespoon of the butter in a small pot along with the garlic, paprika, lemon zest and juice, and salt and pepper. Melt over low heat.

3. Using scissors, cut up the middle of the shell toward the tail, then pull the sides of the shell apart, exposing the meat. Remove the lobster and cut into slightly larger bite-size pieces. Add them to the melted butter to warm.

4. Melt the remaining tablespoon of butter in a small pan over medium heat and add the panko. Mix well to coat the panko with the butter and stir until the crumbs get golden brown, 3 to 4 minutes, then remove from the heat.

5. Combine the celery, celery leaves or parsley, dill, and mayonnaise in a small bowl. Add the lobster (leaving the butter in the pot) and mix well.

6. Fill the toasted bun with the lobster combo, drizzle with a little extra butter from the pot, and add the panko on top at the end.

CHIPOTLE SLOPPY JOE

I'm always amazed at how the addition of the chipotle chile and beer makes this so damn different . . . and way better.

MAKES 4 SANDWICHES

1 tablespoon oil

½ onion, diced small

1 green bell pepper, seeded and diced small

1 pound ground beef

1 large garlic clove, minced

Kosher salt and freshly ground black pepper

2 tablespoons Worcestershire sauce

6 ounces tomato paste

1 cup really good beer (something a little bitter wouldn't be a bad thing here)

3 to 4 chipotle chiles, minced well

4 hamburger-style rolls, or anything you like, really

1. Heat the oil in a large skillet, add the onion and bell pepper, cook for about 3 minutes, then add the ground beef.

2. Continue to cook until the beef is just cooked through, then add the garlic and cook for another minute, or until the garlic is fragrant.

3. Season with salt and black pepper and add the Worcestershire, tomato paste, beer, and chipotles. Mix everything well and then simmer about 10 minutes over medium-low heat until thickened.

4. Serve on the rolls.

BURRITOS

Before we moved to San Diego, a burrito to me was essentially any tortilla with fillings that mostly included rice, beans, and maybe chicken or beef—that's it. Don't get me wrong, because a humble rice and bean burrito would easily warrant a spot on the simplest-but-most-delicious-things-you-should-know-how-to-make list.

But roll the tape forward many years, and burritos to me now are made on large, flour tortillas and are hearty, warm packages of two-handed love filled with all kinds of deliciousness. In fact, a burrito can be so significant in heft, they're often hard to finish in one session . . . said my son Jordan never.

Of course, ours will have the usual suspects: rice, beans, chicken, and beef—but also other great fillings. We'll use fried chicken, old-school Chinese orange chicken, chorizo, and fish sticks—yes, even fish sticks. Some will be finished on the flat top for a crispier outside or wrapped in cheese or bacon (because we can). There may even be a suggestion of repurposing some leftover burrito into amazing French toast.

But before we can get buritto-ing, you'll need to know a few things:

How to Fold a Burrito

You need to know how to fold one because simply using the tortilla as a tube, open on both ends, won't just be wrong, it'll be embarrassing—so pay attention. Oh, sure, there are a couple different ways to fold up a burrito, but this is my fave. And all recipes are based on using a 12-inch flour tortilla.

1. Start by making sure your tortilla is pliable enough to roll, this is *muy importante*—and a quick 15 seconds a side on the flat or 10 seconds in a microwave will do it. Either way, don't miss this step. Then lay it out flat.

2. Put your fillings on the bottom half of the tortilla (the part closest to you).

3. Fold the bottom over the filling and pull back slightly to make it snug.

4. Fold the two sides in toward the center.

5. Roll it up away from you and BOOM—you're a burrito-folding pro!

What to Put in a Burrito

Of course, the recipes that follow are complete, and if you only made them exactly as is, they'd be great. That said, there's a Mexican Rice recipe (page 214) as well as a Refried Beans recipe (page 217)—and just know that you should feel free to add either or both to any burrito you want.

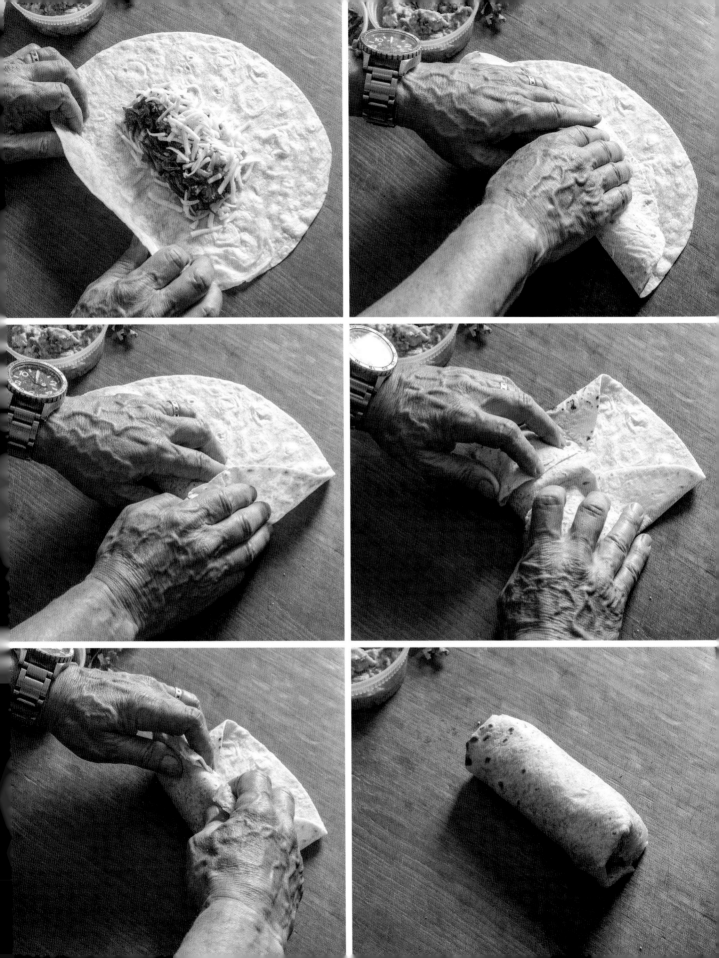

How to Finish the Outside of a Burrito

You have a few options here that can apply to any burrito you'll ever make.

DO NOTHING: I know this sounds lazy AF, but my estimate would be that about 95 percent of the burritos I've eaten or made have had nothing done to them after being filled and rolled—and they were all just straight delicious.

CRISPED ON THE FLAT: Once rolled, it goes into a nonstick pan (or any pan, really) over medium-high heat for color and texture.

CHEESE WRAPPED: Once the burrito has been rolled, scatter a large handful of shredded cheese (enough to cover the outside of the burrito like a blanket) into a rectangle in a nonstick pan over medium-high heat. When the cheese melts and starts to look golden and just starting to get crispy, place the burrito at one end of the rectangle and, using a spatula, lift the cheese and gently roll away to wrap the outside of the burrito, leaving the ends open. And if you want to have real fun, slice some jalapeños superthin and put them on the flat first, then add the cheese. And when you roll it up, oh my . . .

BACON WRAPPED: "Hey, Sam, couldn't you just put bacon *in* the burrito instead of wrapping it?" I won't even dignify that question with a response. Just look at the picture.

How to Eat a Burrito

I know it seems crazy to have to even address this, and for those already acquainted with the process, my apologies. But if you saw one of my Canadian family members trying to eat a taco . . . you'd understand. So, here you go:

- Don't use a knife and fork, ever.
- Don't open it up and eat it like a taco plate, ever.
- If it's wrapped in paper or foil, just unwrap the top inch or so, then pull down from there as necessary. Basically, eat your way across and then down—typewriter style.

Okay, now we can eat.

CALIFORNIA BURRITO

Figured we should start with perhaps the most iconic burrito in San Diego—they say it originated here. By the way, for a classic carne asada burrito, do everything here but leave out the fries or tots.

MAKES 1 BURRITO

1 tortilla

3 to 4 ounces cooked Carne Asada (page 24), warm

⅓ cup shredded cheese (Monterey Jack, Cheddar— any good melting cheese)

1 handful Double-Cooked Fries (page 199), cooked and crispy or 8 Homemade Tots (page 202)

¼ cup Guacamole (page 230)

3 tablespoons Pico de Gallo (page 233)

3 tablespoons Chipotle Lime Sour Cream (page 229)

1. Warm the tortilla, then build: first the carne, then the cheese, the fries or tots, the guacamole, the pico, and finally the chipotle cream.

2. Roll up, brown on the flat . . . then eat.

CHILE RELLENO BURRITO

I've made a lot of burritos, and this one is clearly way near the top. Yes, it's more work than not, but it's so worth it. Plus, you come away knowing how to make a delicious chile relleno.

MAKES 1 BURRITO

1 poblano or pasilla pepper, stem removed (different names, essentially the same thing, though no one really knows)

1 piece of block pepper Jack, cut into a ¾-inch-square piece, about an inch shorter than the pepper, or about ⅓ to ½ cup shredded

Oil for frying

2 large eggs, separated

¾ cup all-purpose flour

1 tortilla

1 cup Mexican Rice (page 214), warmed up

1. Roast the pepper: heat your barbecue grill to high and put the pepper on the grate—you're looking for it to blacken all the way around (this'll probably take 15 minutes), or put it on the grate above an open flame on your stove to blacken it.

2. Either way, when it's there, put it in a paper bag and seal shut, or put it in a bowl and cover tightly with plastic wrap. Leave to steam for 15 minutes, then open and carefully pull off and discard the blackened skin.

3. Make an incision lengthwise down the pepper, but not cutting through the top or bottom. Gently open up and remove the seeds and core—this is best done when the pepper is cool.

4. Then, very carefully, stuff the pepper with the cheese. Set aside.

5. Heat about an inch of oil in a medium pot to 350°F.

6. Put the egg yolks in one bowl and the whites in another.

7. Use a hand blender to whisk the egg yolks smooth and slightly lighter in color.

8. Then, whisk the whites until stiff peaks form, and gently fold them into the yolks mixture. This will be superlight, airy, and foamy.

9. Place the flour in a shallow bowl and roll each stuffed pepper in the flour to cover. Carefully shake off any excess and dip the pepper into the egg mixture to fully coat on both sides.

10. Gently lay the pepper into the hot oil and fry until lightly golden brown on both sides and the cheese has melted, about 5 minutes per side. Then remove from the oil.

11. Warm the tortilla, then add half the rice, the pepper, and the rest of the rice. Roll up.

12. Oh, yes . . .

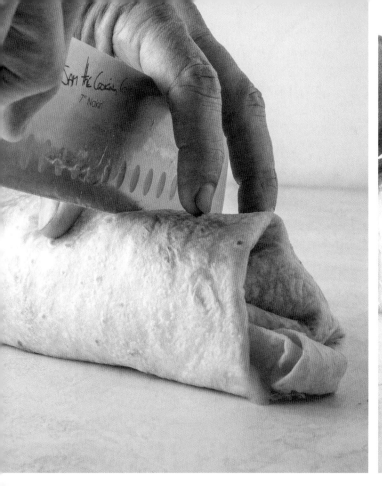

WORTH THE HANGOVER BURRITO

I created this for a charity collaboration in 2021. The name is because it's exactly what the body needs after a rough night. And no, I don't have any scientific proof to back that up, but it's exactly what I would want the morning after. And even if it doesn't help, at least you've just eaten something damn good.

MAKES 1 BURRITO

¼ cup mayonnaise

1 tablespoon sriracha

1 tablespoon maple syrup

Oil

4 ounces sage-flavor ground breakfast sausage, if you can find it (if not, regular breakfast sausage is just fine)

2 large eggs

1 tortilla

⅓ cup Caramelized Onions (page 222)

8 cooked and crispy Homemade Tots (page 202)

⅓ cup shredded Cheddar

1. Combine the mayo, sriracha, and maple syrup in a small bowl. Mix well and set aside. This is your sauce.

2. In a nonstick pan or flat top over medium heat, add a splash of oil, and then the sausage in a ball.

3. Use a spatula to smash flat and let cook until there's a good sear on the bottom. Then flip over and chop (like the Chopped Cheese in the sandwich chapter), and cook until the pink is gone. Remove from the heat and set aside.

4. Cook the eggs—any style, but I suggest over easy because it's all about a runny yolk, but if you've got a hankering for scrambled, go for it.

5. Now let's build: warm tortilla, onions, tots, sausage, cheese, sauce (more is better), and finally the eggs.

6. Roll up and eat away—I wouldn't crisp this one up on the flat because you might cook the eggs more and that could/would be bad.

And since this burrito was based on charity, I thought this would be a good place to mention two charities that are very close to my heart. I've worked with both for many years and try to help every way I can. So feel free to scan the QR codes and send a few dollars their way. You can trust they'll always use the $$ wisely and will appreciate every cent. Plus, you'll end up feeling good (especially after the burrito). Btw, both are tax-exempt 501(c)(3) not-for-profit organizations.

Mama's Kitchen has been home-delivering medically tailored meals at no cost to those with HIV, cancer, congestive heart failure, chronic kidney disease, etc. for more than 30 years. They provide for people who must have proper nourishment to help fight these diseases but are too sick to shop, cook, or prepare meals for themselves. In fact, in March 2021, Mama's celebrated the delivery of their 10 millionth meal.

Noah Homes saw the need 38 years ago for residential-style care for adults with developmental disabilities (before then it was strictly institutional). It's since grown into an amazing community that is a lifetime home to 90 residents. In 2017, they opened two of the first "memory" homes in the country for their residents diagnosed with aging issues, Alzheimer's, or other related dementia.

CHORIZO—MY FAVORITE BURRITO, EVER

At the risk of coming off a bit odd (could be too late, actually), I order the exact same thing from every taco shop I go to—a basic "Chorizo Burrito." Some are great, some are not great—but I love them all. And now I want you to love them, too.

MAKES 1 BURRITO

1 tablespoon oil

½ small onion, diced small

4 ounces Mexican chorizo, pork, beef, or soy sausage—all acceptable choices

2 large eggs

Kosher salt and freshly ground black pepper

⅓ cup shredded Monterey Jack

2 tablespoons sour cream

1 tortilla

¼ cup Refried Beans (page 217)

¼ cup Guacamole (page 230)

Hot sauce (always optional)

1. Heat the oil in a large nonstick pan and add the onion.

2. Cook for about 2 minutes, then add the chorizo, stirring and breaking it up until cooked through, about 5 minutes. Reduce the heat to low.

3. Beat the eggs with a good pinch of salt and pepper and add to the pan with half of the cheese when the chorizo is done.

4. Stir often; you're trying to keep the eggs from drying out.

5. When the eggs are just set, remove from the heat.

6. Build: tortilla, sour cream, refried beans, chorizo mixture, remaining cheese, and guacamole. Add the hot sauce, if using.

7. Roll up and eat.

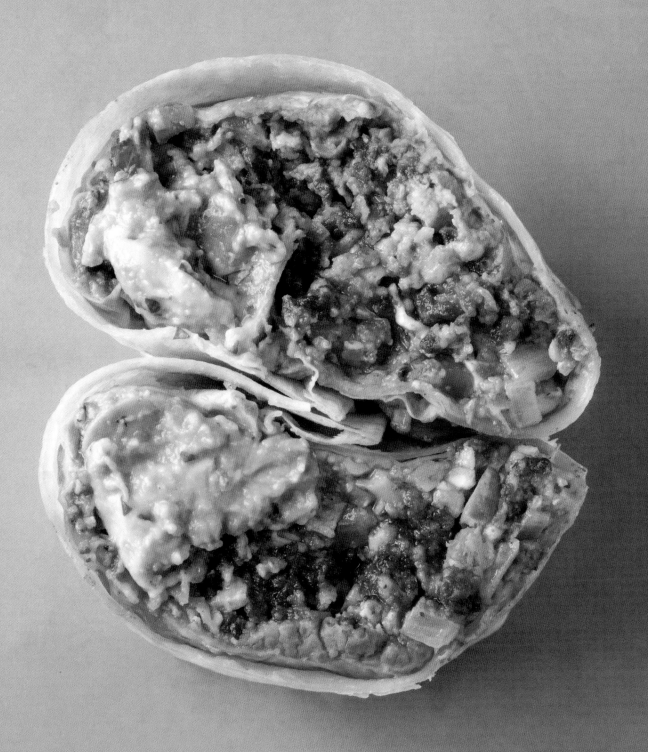

FISH STICK BURRITO

I need to apologize, because in the sandwich chapter I suggested the Grilled PB&J might be the dumbest recipe in this book—and I now realize I might have been wrong. That's because this time we're making a burrito with fish sticks, as in the "little-kid-after-school-eating-frozen-shitty-things-adults-almost-never-eat"—unless they're stoned. Until now, that is. And not bragging, but I believe I've elevated them to proper burrito-worthy status.

MAKES 1 BURRITO

6 frozen fish sticks

1 tortilla

⅓ cup Refried Beans
(page 217), warmed

2 tablespoons Chipotle Lime
Sour Cream (page 229)

2 strips cooked, crispy
bacon, crumbled

⅓ cup shredded Monterey Jack

¼ cup prepared Mexican
Rice (page 214), warmed

2 to 3 tablespoons Pico
de Gallo (page 233)

¼ cup shredded green cabbage

1. Make the fish sticks according to the package directions, or microwave them briefly until no longer frozen (maybe 30 seconds), then crisp them either under the broiler or in a nonstick pan over high heat, turning them a few times.

2. Heat the tortilla just a bit.

3. Build: spoon the beans onto the tortilla, then a layer of the chipotle cream, bacon, fish sticks, cheese, rice, pico, and fresh cabbage. Roll up.

4. Daaaaaamn.

THE OG: RICE, BEAN, AND CHEESE BURRITO

This is easily the warm blanket of the burrito family, and ohhh the comfort. The only difference here is the addition of a roasted poblano pepper—not for heat but for flavor and deliciousness.

MAKES 2 BURRITOS

1 poblano pepper, sliced lengthwise

2 tortillas

Refried Beans (page 217)

Mexican Rice (page 214)

1 cup shredded Cheddar/ Monterey Jack blend

Small handful of tortilla chips

1. Roast the pepper: heat your barbecue grill to high and put the pepper on the grate—you're looking for it to blacken all the way around (this'll probably take 15 minutes), or put it on the grate above an open flame on your stove to blacken it.

2. Either way, when it's there, put it in a paper bag and seal shut, or put it in a bowl and cover with plastic wrap—leave to steam for 15 minutes, then open and carefully pull off and discard the blackened skin.

3. Slice down the middle and remove seeds and membrane, then cut into thin strips.

4. Build: tortilla, layer of refried beans, roasted poblano pepper strips, rice, cheese, another layer of beans, and some tortilla chips. Fold, place on a flat top, and brown on all sides.

NOTE: By the way, one of my all-time favorite, simple, most delicious breakfasts ever is a bowl with Mexican rice on one side, refried beans on the other, topped with a couple beautifully runny fried eggs and garnished with hot sauce and green onions. Straight. Fricking. Heaven.

SURF AND TURF BURRITO

Not sure who first decided that beef and seafood would make great partners, but they deserve a big round of applause for it. And while there's a little marinating involved here, it's pretty much a simple little bundle to throw together . . . a stupidly delicious little bundle. Of course, you could use the carne asada for the "turf" part in this, but now you have another marinade for beef that's really good.

MAKES 4 BURRITOS

2 tablespoons Worcestershire sauce

3 tablespoons soy sauce

2 tablespoons balsamic vinegar

3 tablespoons oil

1 tablespoon Dijon mustard

2 teaspoons honey

2 garlic cloves, minced

1 teaspoon dried rosemary

1 teaspoon kosher salt

1 teaspoon freshly ground black pepper

1 pound skirt steak

1 pound shrimp, peeled and deveined (31/40s are perfect for this)

1 tablespoon sriracha

4 tortillas

1⅓ cups Guacamole (page 230)

1. Put the Worcestershire, 2 tablespoons of the soy sauce, vinegar, 2 tablespoons of the oil, mustard, honey, garlic, rosemary, salt, and pepper in a large zippered bag. Mix well.

2. Add the steak, make sure it's well coated, seal the bag, and refrigerate for a couple of hours.

3. Put the shrimp in a bowl with the remaining tablespoon of soy sauce, the remaining tablespoon of oil, and the sriracha.

4. Coat well and refrigerate.

5. Heat a grill to medium-high, remove the steak from the bag (discard the marinade), and place on the grill.

6. Because it's thin, it won't take very long to cook—likely 2 to 3 minutes per side.

7. When it's done, transfer it to a plate to rest.

8. Now, put on the shrimp, either using a grill wok (they're the best for small stuff like this) or directly on the grill. Cook until done, turning often—only a couple of minutes total—then remove from the grill.

9. Slice the steak across the grain into very thin strips.

10. Build: warm tortilla, guacamole, steak, then shrimp.

11. Roll, then crisp up on a flat top.

LOBSTER BURRITO—PUERTO NUEVO STYLE

Fifty miles south of San Diego is Puerto Nuevo, Mexico, a tiny little handful of streets dedicated to pretty much one thing: lobster. And it's about as simple as can be—deep fried and served with warm tortillas, rice, beans, and melted butter. It's honestly one of the greatest things ever. Everything gets loaded up in a tortilla and off you go.

MAKES 1 BURRITO

One 5- to 6-ounce
  uncooked lobster tail
Oil
2 tablespoons salted butter
1 garlic clove, minced
Pinch of smoked paprika
1 tortilla
⅓ cup Refried Beans (page 217)
⅓ cup Mexican Rice (page 214)

1. Steam the lobster tail or put in simmering water for 3 minutes, then remove and put into ice water to stop the cooking.

2. Using scissors, cut up the middle of the shell toward the tail, then pull the sides of the shell apart, exposing the meat. Use a knife to cut down to, but not through, the breastplate . . . or whatever it's called. Dry the tail well.

3. Heat about an inch of oil in a small pot to 350°F and add the tail. Cook for a couple of minutes until opaque. Transfer to paper towels to drain, then cut into bite-size pieces.

4. Melt the butter with the garlic and paprika.

5. Warm the tortilla and build: tortilla, refried beans, lobster, drizzle with butter, then add the rice. Roll up and serve with extra butter for your bites.

6. Excellente.

ORANGE CHICKEN BURRITO

Panda Express is a Chinese fast-food place that used to be in a supermarket close to our house, and an order of orange chicken on rice was our kids' favorite after-school snack. We don't remember where the suggestion for this burrito version came from, but it's a good one.

MAKES 4 BURRITOS

Oil

1 pound boneless, skinless chicken thighs

2 large eggs, beaten

½ cup all-purpose flour

½ cup cornstarch

2 oranges

1 tablespoon honey

½ cup light brown sugar

3 tablespoons soy sauce

2 tablespoons rice vinegar

1 tablespoon grated fresh ginger

1 garlic clove, minced

1 tablespoon cornstarch plus 2 tablespoons water

1½ cups cooked white rice

4 tortillas

¼ cup diced green onions

1 teaspoon toasted sesame seeds

Sriracha

1. Heat about an inch or so of oil in a small pot to 350°F.

2. Cut the chicken into equal-size small chunks.

3. Put the eggs in one shallow bowl. Stir together the flour and cornstarch in another.

4. Bread the chicken: first into the flour mixture, shaking off the excess; next, into the egg; and then back into the flour, being sure the chicken is well covered.

5. Carefully put into the oil and cook until done, 4 to 5 minutes or an internal temp of 165°F. Then transfer to paper towels to drain.

6. While the chicken cooks, combine the zest of one of the oranges, the juice of both, and the honey, brown sugar, soy sauce, vinegar, ginger, and garlic in a small pot. Stir well to mix and bring to a low simmer.

7. Mix the tablespoon of cornstarch with the water in a small bowl until smooth, then stir into the orange sauce to thicken. When thick, add the chicken and stir to coat with the sauce.

8. Build: put a layer of the rice on the tortilla, then the chicken, green onions, sesame seeds, and sriracha to taste.

9. Roll, then heat on a flat top until evenly golden brown on all sides.

WET BEEF BURRITO

I realize the term *wet* doesn't sound all that appealing, and I give you kudos for even getting this far. A regular burrito you eat with your hands, but a wet burrito has sauce and cheese on top and is generally a knife-and-fork proposition. And this one has meltingly tender shredded beef inside. Any extra can be frozen, allowing you to make these on a moment's notice.

MAKES 6 TO 8 BURRITOS

One 3-pound chuck roast

Oil

1 red bell pepper, seeded and roughly chopped

1 green bell pepper, seeded and roughly chopped

1 small yellow onion, roughly chopped

2 tablespoons roughly chopped chipotle chile

1 teaspoon garlic powder

1 teaspoon ground cumin

1 teaspoon chipotle chile powder

1 teaspoon dried oregano

1 tablespoon kosher salt

1 cup beef stock

6 to 8 tortillas

Shredded Monterey Jack cheese

Green salsa (store-bought)

Red enchilada sauce (store-bought)

Sour cream

Fresh cilantro

1. Set your pressure cooker to BROWN or SAUTÉ.

2. Cut the meat into 5 or 6 pieces, remove excess fat (some is just fine), lightly oil, then sear the meat in the cooker until browned on all sides. You might need to do this in batches because if it's too packed, the temp will come way down and it won't brown.

3. Put all the meat back into the cooker and add the bell peppers, onion, chipotle, garlic powder, cumin, chipotle chile powder, oregano, salt, and beef stock.

4. Close the lid, set it to high pressure, and cook for 1 hour. When done, allow the pressure to release naturally.

5. Transfer to a large bowl and shred—and try not to eat everything right now.

6. For each burrito, warm a tortilla, add ¼ cup of cheese, 4 ounces of the shredded beef, 2 tablespoons of green salsa, and another ¼ cup of cheese, then roll.

7. Preheat the oven to 400°F, then put each burrito, seam side down, on a greased baking sheet, brush the burrito lightly with oil, and bake until golden, about 25 minutes.

8. Turn the oven to BROIL, add more cheese to the top, and put back in until melted—just a minute or so—then remove from the broiler.

9. Put some warmed enchilada sauce on a plate, place the burrito on top, then add a little sour cream on top with more green salsa and a final garnish of fresh cilantro.

DOGS

Sausage, frankfurter, wiener, footlong, tube steak, red hot, and even weenie—the simple hot dog has many nicknames. And while the origins of it are not exactly cemented in history (let's just say the origin story could have many versions), our love for them is absolute. In fact, my wife, Kelly, is such a fan that to her even a crappy dog is still a delicious dog.

And because dogs can be an immensely personal thing, there's no hope of our agreeing on which ones to use. I mean, look at the lineup: jumbo, skinless, all beef, uncured, chicken, turkey (okay, maybe those last two are a stretch), kosher, wagyu, natural, snappy casing, and more. But even if you're a creature of hot dog habit, I suggest you branch out a bit and try new ones from time to time.

But before we get going, here are the chapter rules:

WHEN I SAY *DOG*: Use whatever you like. I'll use a variety so the pictures are pretty and I don't get bored (take that as a hint for your own hot dog life).

WHEN I SAY *BUN*: Same thing as the dog.

WHEN I SAY *COOK*: You do you and do whatever you like because you have free rein here. (But for information, see "How to Cook a Dog" on page 178). Same goes for the bun.

Okay, I think that's it. I could definitely go on, but the only way we get anywhere is if I shut up and start the recipes.

How to Cook a Dog

Even though they're already fully cooked, I'm guessing we can't even agree on how to cook them. Because, once again, there are many options:

SIMMERING: Depending on size, anywhere from 4 to 6 minutes.

OVEN: Bake at 400°F for 10 to 15 minutes, or until they sizzle.

MICROWAVE: Please just don't.

PANFRY: In a nonstick pan over high heat until perfectly browned all the way around.

SLOW COOKER: What a waste of time; forget it.

ON THE GRILL: 3 to 4 minutes until awesome.

DEEP FRIED: Crazy delicious—heat about ½ inch of oil in a small pot or pan (big enough to hold the dog, of course) to 350°F and cook the dog for 2 to 3 minutes total, turning often.

OR MY FAVE COMBO OF SIMMERING AND PANFRYING: I simmer the dogs for about 3 minutes, then throw them in a nonstick pan over high heat or on the grill and cook until done. Perfection.

But wait, this is superimportant: I also like to make small slits in them that open during cooking and create way more crispy edges.

How to Warm a Bun

And let's not forget the buns—because a hot dog bun should *never* be served cold:

Toasted

Broiled

Grilled

Pan-fried

Buttered then pan-fried

Over the campfire

Steamed

SOUR CREAM AND GREEN ONION DOG

I heard once that this was popular in Seattle, so I made it and loved it. Then I heard it was cream cheese they eat in Seattle, not sour cream, but I still loved it. The sour cream is light and really good, especially with the green onions. And it has nothing to do with my green onion obsession, I don't think. It's really more of the simple combo and how it just fricking works.

MAKES 1 DOG

1 dog

1 bun

3 tablespoons sour cream

¼ cup diced green onion
(more is better)

1. Cook the dog and bun.

2. Spread the sour cream on the bun, then add the dog and finally the green onions.

3. Resist the urge to add anything else; it's just wonderful by itself.

PEPPERONI DOG

Who says because it's pepperoni, you must have a pizza sauce? Well, certainly not me, because I ain't using it. This is all about simple . . . and totally delicious.

MAKES 1 DOG

⅓ cup mini pepperoni

1 dog

1 bun

1 tablespoon Garlic Aioli (page 229)

3 tablespoons Western-style chili sauce

⅓ cup shredded mozzarella

¼ teaspoon dried oregano

1. Turn the broiler to high.
2. In a nonstick pan over medium-high heat, add the pepperoni and cook until the fat renders and the peps begin to cup up a bit.
3. Cook the dog.
4. Open the bun and put under the broiler to get just a bit crispy.
5. Put the garlic aioli and chili sauce on the bun.
6. Then add the dog and the mozzarella.
7. Put back under broiler to just melt the cheese.
8. Remove from the broiler, add the pepperoni, and sprinkle with oregano.
9. Go to town.

GREEK DOG

Tzatziki is one of those things that makes everything better—and this dog is no exception. It's cool, it's garlicky and lemony, and it's a tremendous change. And unless you're Greek, it won't make you feel patriotic the way a chili dog can do in the USA, but you'll feel great . . . which is almost the same thing.

MAKES 4 DOGS

½ cup plain Greek yogurt

1 cup grated cucumber (about ½ medium cucumber), squeezed in a towel to get rid of as much moisture as possible

1 garlic clove, minced

1 tablespoon chopped fresh dill

1 tablespoon fresh lemon juice

Kosher salt

1 tablespoon olive oil

¼ cup diced tomato

¼ cup Kalamata olives, pitted and diced small

1 tablespoon finely chopped fresh parsley

1 teaspoon red wine vinegar

4 hot dogs

4 buns

2 tablespoons crumbled feta for garnish

1. Combine the yogurt, cucumber, garlic, dill, lemon juice, salt to taste, and olive oil in a small bowl and mix well; this is your tzatziki.

2. Combine the tomato, olives, parsley, and vinegar in a separate small bowl. Season with salt and mix well, then set aside.

3. Make small diagonal slits on all sides of the dogs and cook in a nonstick pan over medium heat until browned and crispy.

4. Build: bun, tzatziki, hot dog, tomato mixture.

5. Garnish with feta.

6. Eat, dance with towels in your hands, and throw plates into the fireplace.

WIENERS AND BEANS AND CHIPS DOG

Oh yes, this is one of those laughable combinations that ceases to be funny after one bite. And while it probably won't dethrone apple pie as the most Americana-esque food out there, the combo of hot dog, baked beans, and potato chips has gotta be a close second— no? I pledge allegiance to this hot dog, and to the deliciousness it brings . . .

MAKES 1 DOG

1 hot dog, split lengthwise
    with a hinge before cooking
    (this would be a good time
    for a quarter-pounder)

1 bun

2 tablespoons mayonnaise

¼ cup Bacony Baked
    Beans (page 209)

2 tablespoons diced white onion

Small pile of crushed potato chips

1. Cook the dog and bun accordingly.

2. Build: mayo on the bun, then the dog, then the beans, the onion, and finally the chips.

THE HAWAIIAN DOG

I used to be a Hawaiian pizza hater, but one good bite a few years ago changed all that. It was the idea of hot fruit that threw me. Not anymore, though, because now I'm a fan—and for those who don't like the idea, I say it's time to grow up and accept the deliciousness before you.

MAKES 2 DOGS

2 tablespoons oil, plus more as needed

¼ red onion, sliced thinly

2 dogs, sliced down the middle, leaving a hinge— a.k.a. butterflied

2 slices fresh pineapple, each about 2 by 5 inches by ½ inch thick

2 buns

3 tablespoons mayonnaise

2 tablespoons teriyaki sauce or marinade (look for a thick one)

1½ teaspoons sriracha

4 strips cooked, crispy bacon, crumbled

1. Heat the oil in a pan large enough for the dogs, then cook the red onion over medium heat for about 15 minutes, or until beautifully softened. Remove from the heat and set aside.

2. Increase the heat to medium-high, add a little more oil, and then the dogs and pineapple. Cook until each is getting some great color (doing this on a grill wouldn't hurt).

3. Remove the dogs from the pan and chop pineapple into ¼-inch cubes.

4. Build: bun, mayo, teriyaki sauce, sriracha, hot dog, onion, pineapple, bacon.

CHILI DOG

The epicenter of the hot dog world, no? And sometimes we like to get a slightly larger bun and then double up on the dogs—the rest stays as is, it's just way hot-doggier.

MAKES 2 DOGS

¾ cup premade hash browns or 1 small, peeled potato and a couple tablespoons of oil

2 hot dogs

2 hot dog buns

⅓ cup Cheese Whiz

¼ cup sour cream

½ cup Burger/Hot Dog Chili (page 221), heated

1. Heat the hash browns (if using) until hot and crispy.

2. Alternatively, grate the potato into a bowl of water, let sit a minute or so, and stir around a bit to remove any excess starch.

3. Heat the oil in a medium pan over medium heat.

4. Rinse and drain the potatoes, dry really well, and add to the pan. Over the next 10 minutes of stirring often, they will become tiny, crispy morsels of greatness. Remove from the heat and set aside.

5. Cook the dogs and buns your favorite way.

6. Warm the Cheez Whiz in a microwave until pourable, then build: bun, sour cream, chili, dogs, cheese drizzle, then hash browns.

BACON-WRAPPED ELOTE DOG

This dog is two of my favorite Mexican food things all wrapped up in one. My first bacon-wrapped dog was when leaving a Lakers game in Los Angeles one night. Do I remember the score or who they played? Nope. But I can almost remember the face of the hot dog man outside the Staples Center who made my dog . . .

MAKES 4 DOGS

4 strips uncooked bacon
4 dogs
4 buns
⅓ cup mayonnaise
1 cup Elote Corn Salad (page 213)

1. Wrap the bacon diagonally around the dog and give it a little press with your fingers at the ends.

2. Alternatively, you could always use toothpicks to keep the bacon in place until it cooks—but for me that feels like training wheels, and I'd rather struggle than use them (but that's just me).

3. Cook the dog on something flat—it'll just cook more evenly than on a grill, and you want the bacon to have an even crisp all the way around.

4. Cook the buns the way you like, and when ready, build: bun, some mayo, the dog, and some of the corn salad.

CORN BRATS

A corn dog is one of the great food joys in life, and a trip to the fair would be sadly incomplete without one. And as good as they are, a corn brat is on a whole different level. They're just that much more interesting.

MAKES 4 BRATS

Oil for frying
¾ cup cornmeal
¾ cup all-purpose flour
1½ teaspoons baking powder
½ teaspoon baking soda
½ teaspoon kosher salt
2 tablespoons white sugar
1 teaspoon chipotle chile powder
2 large eggs
¾ cup buttermilk
4 fully cooked bratwurst
Cornstarch for dredging

1. Put about an inch of oil into a medium pot and heat to 350°F.

2. Stir together the cornmeal, flour, baking powder, baking soda, salt, sugar, and chile powder in a large bowl.

3. Beat the eggs in a small bowl and stir in the buttermilk.

4. Pour the egg mixture into the dry ingredients and thoroughly mix into a thick batter. Transfer to a tall, narrow glass (trust me).

5. Insert a wooden skewer or stick (even a chopstick) about halfway into each of the brats.

6. This next part is optional, but I really like it: on a flat griddle or in large nonstick pan over medium-high heat, sear the brats so they start to get a little golden all the way around—this should only take a couple of minutes. Then dry them off well.

7. Spread some cornstarch on a plate and lightly roll each brat in the cornstarch.

8. Using the skewer as a handle, dunk the brats all the way into the batter, turning it as you go and swirling it around on the way out. Gently place the brats in the hot oil.

9. While they are cooking, give them a little turn so the whole thing gets some facedown time in the oil. Cook until golden, 3 to 4 minutes. Will they be perfectly cylindrical like the places with special corn dog machines? No. But that's okay, it really is.

10. Remove from the oil, drain off any excess oil on paper towels, and let cool for a bit before eating.

SIDES, SAUCES, AND STUFF

This chapter doesn't really need much of an introduction, other than to say a dog, a burger, and even a taco by itself is fine—but adding something on the side? Now that's being a good host . . . even if you're just cooking for you.

Double-Cooked
Fries

Garlic Fries

Buffalo
Chicken Fries

DOUBLE-COOKED FRIES

The double cooking gives you the perfectly crispy fry of your dreams. And you can always cook them the first time well before—then just give them the ol' second cook when you need them.

MAKES 2 POUNDS OF FRIES

2 pounds russet potatoes

Oil for frying

Kosher salt

A word about oil: Pretty much any oil will work: avocado, vegetable, canola, even peanut—although peanut will likely be the most expensive. And I'd definitely stay away from flavored oils, like olive and extra virgin olive oil, cuz they're just not necessary.

1. Rinse and scrub the potatoes and peel them if you prefer, but it's not necessary.

2. Slice into planks lengthwise and then into sticks roughly ¼ by ¼ inch, then put them in a bowl of cold water to keep them from turning brown—this will also help remove any excess starch. Let them soak up to an hour.

3. When ready, drain the potatoes on paper towels really, really, really well because wet fries and hot oil are nothing you want to be involved with.

4. Fill a deep fryer or large, heavy pot with about 3 inches of oil and heat to 325°F.

5. Cook the fries in batches for 5 minutes. Note: Do not crowd the pot with too many fries—a crowded pot is *no bueno*. Remove them and drain on fresh paper towels—they won't be brown or crispy at this point.

6. Once all the potatoes have been cooked, increase the oil temp to 400°F and cook a second time until they're golden and crisp.

7. Remove from the oil, drain again on paper towels, put in a bowl, immediately sprinkle with salt, and go for it.

GARLIC FRIES

Now that you have great fries, let's make them even better.

MAKES 2 POUNDS OF FRIES

¼ cup salted butter

6 garlic cloves, finely minced

Double-Cooked Fries (page 199)

3 tablespoons finely
  chopped fresh parsley

⅓ cup shredded Parmesan

Kosher salt

1. Melt the butter any way you want and stir in the garlic.

2. Put the cooked fries in a large bowl and drizzle with the melted garlic butter.

3. Toss well, adding parsley and cheese as you go, making sure all fries get mixed well.

4. Sprinkle with a touch of salt and serve.

BUFFALO CHICKEN FRIES

I like the buffalo sauce, honey, and butter combo so much, I've made these without chicken . . . and hardly missed it. Then again, I've made it with fried chicken, such as in the Nashville Hot Chicken Taco, and it was nuts. You've got some options, I'm saying.

MAKES 2 POUNDS OF FRIES

2 boneless, skinless chicken thighs or the chicken from the Nashville Hot Chicken Taco recipe (page 41)

Oil

Kosher salt and freshly ground black pepper

½ cup Frank's RedHot Original Cayenne Pepper Sauce

¼ cup honey

2 tablespoons salted butter

1 batch Double-Cooked Fries (page 199)

⅓ cup blue cheese salad dressing

Chopped celery leaves or fresh parsley for garnish

1. Remove the chicken from fridge 30 minutes before cooking, lightly oil, season with salt and pepper, and put on the grill.

2. Cook until well marked with an internal temp of 160 to 165°F. Remove from the grill and chop up into bite-sized pieces.

3. To create a sauce, stir together the hot sauce, honey, and butter in a small pot over low heat.

4. Toss the fries with some of the sauce (don't oversauce), then put on a platter, add the chicken, drizzle with blue cheese dressing, and top with celery leaves.

5. Eat the hell out of it.

HOMEMADE TOTS

We made these tots for our YouTube channel and, as soon as we finished the video, we started eating them and didn't stop till they were all gone. A fresh, crispy, just-out-of-the-oil tot is amazing—but then when you dip 'em in a sauce? Oh man . . .

MAKES APPROXIMATELY 24 TOTS

2 large russet potatoes
Oil for frying
1 tablespoon all-purpose flour
1 teaspoon garlic powder
1 teaspoon dried oregano
½ teaspoon onion powder
½ teaspoon smoked paprika
½ teaspoon each kosher salt and freshly ground pepper

1. Peel the potatoes, place in a small pot, cover with cold water, and put on the stove over medium-high heat.

2. Bring to a boil and let cook for about 6 minutes—you want them only tender enough that a knife or skewer can go in about ¼ inch—then rinse with cold water and set aside.

3. When the potatoes have cooled, grate them into a bowl using the large holes of a box grater. If your potatoes have a lot of moisture, put the grated potatoes in a large kitchen towel and squeeze out the excess moisture.

4. Heat about an inch of oil in the bottom of a cast-iron pan or pot to 350°F.

5. Combine the flour, garlic powder, oregano, onion powder, paprika, salt, and pepper. Mix well with your hands.

6. Shape into tots; you should end up with anywhere from 20 to 30 tots. Btw, I find a light coating of oil on your hands helps this go much easier.

7. Carefully put the tots into the oil and let cook until golden brown, turning over as necessary.

8. When done, drain on paper towels, and then season lightly with salt.

CRISPY ONIONS

Almost any onion does it for me, but these little guys hold a special place in my stomach. But remember, use them often and on anything—I mean everything.

MAKES AS MANY AS YOU NEED (OR CAN EAT)

1 large yellow onion, sliced in half, then into thin half-moons

1½ cups buttermilk

2 cups all-purpose flour

2 tablespoons smoked or regular paprika

2 to 3 cups oil for frying

Kosher salt and freshly ground black pepper

1. Put the sliced onion and buttermilk in a large bowl; be sure all the onion is covered.

2. Combine the flour and paprika in a separate large bowl. Stir well, then remove the onion from the buttermilk, shake off any excess, and drop the onion into the flour mixture, making sure all the onion slices get evenly covered.

3. Heat the oil in a medium pot to 350°F.

4. Carefully put the dredged onion into the hot oil, separating the pieces as you go. Give them a gentle stir to keep them from clumping together and cook until golden brown and crispy, 2 to 3 minutes. Transfer to paper towels to drain any excess oil.

5. Season with salt, pepper, or both. Sometimes just a bunch of pepper is a nice change.

CRISPY SHREDDED POTATOES

We took a shortcut and made these instead of matchstick potatoes while we were shooting in Miami, and boy were we glad we did—cuz they are fricking great.

MAKES ABOUT 1½ CUPS

Oil for frying
1 large russet potato

1. In a medium pot, heat about ½ inch of the oil to 350°F.

2. Peel the potato and then shred, using the large holes of a box grater. Put the grated potato into cold water to keep from browning.

3. Drain and dry the potatoes. Gently place the potatoes in the oil and cook until golden brown, 2 to 3 minutes.

4. Remove to paper towels to drain and then eat.

BACONY BAKED BEANS

This can go with pretty much anything in this book, and honestly should. We serve these at Samburgers and people love them. Plus, they can easily be made a day or two or three in advance and will still be awesome.

MAKES ABOUT 6 SERVINGS

10 ounces uncooked bacon, diced

½ yellow onion, diced small

½ green bell pepper, diced small

One 28-ounce can baked beans (the maple ones are great here)

¼ cup chili sauce (like Heinz, not the spicy version)

1 tablespoon prepared yellow mustard

1½ teaspoons Worcestershire sauce

2 tablespoons pure maple syrup

2 tablespoons light brown sugar

1 to 2 chipotle chiles, minced (maybe start with 1)

Big pinch of kosher salt

Chopped green onions for garnish

1. Preheat the oven to 350°F.

2. Cook the bacon in an ovenproof pot with a lid until about halfway done; leave the bacon in the pot, removing all but 2 tablespoons of the fat.

3. Add the onion and bell pepper and cook until both are softened and the bacon is just about getting crispy—about 5 minutes.

4. Add all the remaining ingredients except the green onions, stir well to mix, then cover and bake for about 45 minutes, or until bubbly.

5. Garnish with green onions to serve.

NO MAYO POTATO SALAD

Everyone needs a good potato salad recipe, especially one without mayo because we all have that one friend who refuses to eat mayo—right, Jill? Or who *claims* not to like it but you're convinced is a closet mayo lover. Plus, a mayo-based dish sitting in the sun outside at a picnic or barbecue can be hazardous to your health. But you can enjoy this one anywhere, anytime . . . especially late night with some toast and the glow of the refrigerator light illuminating the moment. Wait, did I just say that out loud?

MAKES ABOUT 6 SERVINGS

2 pounds red and yellow
    new potatoes, skin on

2 celery stalks, diced

3 tablespoons chopped
    fresh parsley

2 tablespoons chopped fresh dill

10 slices cooked, crispy
    bacon, diced

3 tablespoons honey

3 tablespoons Dijon mustard

2 garlic cloves, crushed

Juice of 1 lemon

Kosher salt and freshly
    ground black pepper

6 hard-boiled eggs, peeled
    and quartered

1. Cook the potatoes in boiling water until soft enough for a fork to pierce easily.

2. Rinse with cold water, and when cool enough to handle, quarter them and place in a large bowl with the celery, parsley, dill, and bacon.

3. Combine the honey, mustard, garlic, lemon juice, and salt and pepper to taste in a small bowl. Mix well, then add as much as you like to the bowl of potatoes and toss.

4. Gently mix in the eggs, season with a little more salt and a lot more pepper, and serve.

ELOTE CORN SALAD

Grilled corn deliciousness—this could (and should) become your new favorite summertime salad.

MAKES 4 EARS

8 tablespoons (1 stick)
  salted butter

1 tablespoon chili powder

Juice of 1 lime (make it a juicy one)

Kosher salt

2 tablespoons oil

4 ears fresh corn, husks
  and silk yanked off

2 tablespoons mayonnaise,
  preferably Japanese
  Kewpie brand

1 large garlic clove, minced

Zest and juice of 1 lime

½ teaspoon chipotle chile powder

⅓ cup crumbled cotija or
  feta or even Parmesan

¼ cup finely chopped
  fresh cilantro

1. Preheat a grill to medium-high.

2. Combine the butter, chili powder, lime juice, and ½ teaspoon of salt in a small pot, and if the pot doesn't have any plastic, put it right on the grill to melt. If it has plastic, use the stovetop.

3. Lighlty oil all the ears, put them on the grill, and cook maybe 10 minutes or until the corn starts getting some burn spots—you want this.

4. You now want to baste every few minutes or so, and you want the corn to soften nicely as well as get some good grill marks—this will take about 20 minutes.

5. When done, remove from the grill and let the corn cool.

6. Cut the kernels off the cob. Put them into a large bowl along with the mayo, garlic, lime zest and juice, and chipotle chile powder. Mix well, then add the cheese and cilantro.

7. Taste, add more salt if necessary, and serve or refrigerate until ready to use.

MEXICAN RICE

Cooking white or brown rice is a basic skill everyone should have. But now you'll also be able to bust out simple and delicious Mexican rice. Way to go, amigo—your friends and family are going to love you.

MAKES ABOUT 3 CUPS

Oil

½ small yellow onion, diced

1 cup uncooked long-
   grain white rice

1 teaspoon garlic powder

1 teaspoon dried oregano

1 teaspoon ground cumin

1 teaspoon salt

1¾ cups chicken stock

½ cup tomato sauce

1. Heat a little oil over medium heat in a small pot and cook the onion for about 5 minutes. Then add the rice and cook until slightly toasted—about 5 minutes more.

2. Add the garlic powder, oregano, cumin, and salt. Mix, and then add the stock and tomato sauce.

3. Stir well to combine, bring to a boil, cover, lower the heat, and simmer for 15 to 18 minutes.

4. Turn off the heat and let sit 10 for minutes, then fluff and serve.

5. Fluff, ha ha.

REFRIED BEANS

Refried beans could very easily be part of my last meal. And for me, there's almost nothing they don't go with. My fave though might be with eggs and fresh tortillas for breakfast—they're kind of stupendous.

MAKES 4 TO 6 SERVINGS

Oil

½ cup finely diced yellow or white onion

One 28-ounce can pinto beans, drained but reserve the liquid

½ teaspoon garlic powder

½ teaspoon ground cumin

½ teaspoon salt

1. Heat about 1½ teaspoons of oil in a small pot, add the onion, and cook until just beginning to soften, maybe 5 minutes.

2. Add the drained beans and ½ cup of the liquid from the beans, stir well, and bring to a simmer. Leave on a low simmer for 5 minutes.

3. Add the garlic powder, cumin, and salt, stir, then mash the beans to your desired consistency (mine is a little chunky and a little smooth), adding more liquid as necessary.

4. Serve.

FRICKLES (FRIED DILL PICKLES)

Just your basic, crunchy, über-delicious accompaniment. Which, if you've never had, you've definitely been missing out.

MAKES 6 SERVINGS, OR IF IT'S ME, JUST 1

½ cup mayonnaise

1 teaspoon chili powder

Juice of ½ lime

1 garlic clove, crushed

2 cups all-purpose flour

3 large eggs, beaten

2 cups panko bread crumbs

Kosher salt and freshly ground black pepper

Oil for frying

6 whole dill pickles, quartered into spears, or sixths if they're large

1. Combine the mayo, chili powder, lime juice, and garlic in a small bowl, mix together, then set aside to be your dipping sauce.

2. Put the flour, eggs, and panko in three separate bowls. Season the panko with salt and pepper to taste, stirring to incorporate.

3. Heat at least an inch of oil in a pot or cast-iron pan to 350°F.

4. Coat each pickle with the flour, shaking off any excess, then into the egg, then back to the flour, then the egg again, and finally in the seasoned panko—be sure to coat well.

5. Fry a few spears at a time until golden brown, about 3 minutes, then transfer to paper towels to drain.

6. Finish the fried pickles with a little salt as they come out of the fryer and serve with dipping sauce.

BURGER/HOT DOG CHILI

There's a definite difference to me between burger/hot dog chili and regular chili. To me, regular chili has beans and big chunks of meat and/or veggies—not this one. This is just meat and seasonings and is way delicious, but it doesn't overpower any burger or dog it's on. You could say this chili knows its place.

SERVES 6

Oil

1 pound ground beef

1 teaspoon onion powder

1 teaspoon garlic powder

1 tablespoon chili powder

8 ounces tomato sauce

2 tablespoons ketchup

1 tablespoon Dijon mustard

1 tablespoon minced chipotle chile

1 tablespoon Worcestershire sauce

½ cup beef or chicken stock

Kosher salt to taste

1. Heat a tablespoon of oil in a large pan over medium-high heat, add the beef, and cook until no longer pink.

2. Stir in the onion, garlic, chili powder, tomato sauce, ketchup, mustard, chipotle, and Worcestershire and mix well.

3. Add the stock and salt, stir superwell, and then keep at a low simmer until the chili thickens up and is no longer a soupy mess, about 15 minutes.

CARAMELIZED ONIONS

If the only thing you get out of this book is this recipe, it'll still be worth it. Because there's almost nothing that gorgeously caramelized onions can't make better.

MAKES ABOUT 1 CUP ONIONS

2 large yellow onions, peeled
2 tablespoons salted butter
2 tablespoons oil
Kosher salt

1. Cut both onions in half through the root end, then cut across into thin slices—it's going to look like a lot, but you'll end up with way less because of shrinkage (and yes, I'm a *Seinfeld* fan).

2. Melt the butter and oil in a large, wide pan over medium heat, then add the onions and about a teaspoon of salt.

3. Cook the onions, stirring to make sure they don't stick but also get even exposure to the bottom of the pan.

4. You're going for golden brown (see pic), and this only comes from medium heat and time—too much heat and it burns, too little heat and nothing happens and you'll want to poke your eyes out. But stick with me because it's so damn worth it.

5. Remember to stir to keep from getting too much color in one spot—in all, this can take anywhere from 30 to 45 minutes.

6. If you find the onions drying out too much, add a little more butter or oil and you'll be fine.

7. When they're there, use them right away or refrigerate them. But if you fridge them, for sure warm them up before using.

NOTE: If you're feeling a little frisky, feel free to add any of the following at about the halfway point:
- A teaspoon or so of any fresh herb—thyme and rosemary would be wonderful.
- Vinegar—a tablespoon of balsamic for some sweetness, or even a little cider vinegar for more of a tangy-get-you-in-the-jaw punch.
- Brown sugar—when you want more sweetness.
- Beer or vermouth—a nice little ¼-cup splash of either three-quarters of the way through will eventually evaporate off, leaving behind a hint of their amazing flavor.
- Lots of freshly ground black pepper—I especially love this on a brat or dog.
- A squeeze or two of a grainy mustard.

BACON ONION JAM

It's thick, it's rich, and it's jammy . . . in a bacon-esque sort of way. But the real point is that this can go on almost anything and should. And while I realize there's no avocado toast creations in this book, it would be ideal under the avocado on one you might make. Just a hidden, delicious treat.

MAKES 2½ CUPS

1 pound uncooked maple bacon, chopped small

1 red onion, finely chopped

2 garlic cloves, minced

1 large tomato, finely chopped (about 1 cup)

⅓ cup cider vinegar

½ teaspoon cayenne pepper

½ teaspoon freshly ground black pepper

½ cup apricot jam

1. Cook the bacon in a large pan until about three-quarters done; when it starts getting superfoamy, you know you're there.

2. Remove three-quarters of the grease (save for something else), add the red onion, and mix well.

3. Cook for 3 to 4 minutes, then add the garlic and stir through for about a minute. Add stir in the tomato and let simmer about 10 minutes, stirring occasionally.

4. Add the vinegar, cayenne, black pepper, and jam. Stir well to combine, turn the heat down to low, and leave it mostly alone for 10 to 15 minutes, stirring occasionally.

5. Transfer to a bowl and use right away or refrigerate, but at least bring to room temp before using.

Curry
Ketchup

Honey
Mustard

Burger
Sauce

Chipotle
Lime Sour
Cream

Hoisin-Chili
Sauce

Garlic
Aioli

CURRY KETCHUP

Anyone who's been to Germany has almost definitely had currywurst: a cut-up sausage served with kind of a curry ketchup. This is a supereasy, two-ingredient version of curry ketchup that you'll be happy you know about.

MAKES ABOUT ⅓ CUP

⅓ cup ketchup
2 teaspoons curry powder

1. Combine both ingredients in a small bowl.
2. Mix well and refrigerate until ready to use.

HONEY MUSTARD

It's late and I can't think of much to say other than this is better than buying it.

MAKES ABOUT ⅓ CUP

¼ cup mayonnaise
1½ tablespoons Dijon mustard
2 tablespoons hot honey—
   regular honey is fine too
Salt and pepper

1. Combine all ingredients in a small bowl.
2. Mix well and refrigerate until ready to use.

BURGER SAUCE

Everyone needs a good burger sauce. And just because it says burger, doesn't mean it's only for burgers. Seriously.

MAKES ABOUT A CUP

½ cup mayonnaise

3 tablespoons dill pickle, diced very small

2 tablespoons ketchup

1 tablespoon sriracha

1½ teaspoons prepared yellow mustard

Pinch each of kosher salt and freshly ground black pepper

1. Put everything into a small bowl and mix to combine.
2. Use it.

HOISIN—CHILI SAUCE

I'm constantly preaching the benefits of keeping a handful of Asian condiments around. This is a perfect example of how two of the most common ones make an uncommon change to your food world.

MAKES ABOUT ½ CUP

¼ cup mayo

2 tablespoons hoisin sauce

1 to 2 tablespoons garlic chili sauce

1. Combine all ingredients in a small bowl.
2. Mix well and refrigerate until ready to use.

CHIPOTLE LIME SOUR CREAM

This can go on a bunch of things, including a shrimp taco I've been making forever. Anyway, a family member asked for this recipe years ago, but instead of using one chipotle, he used an entire *can* of chipotles. Suffice it to say the recipient was still trying to cool his mouth down an hour later.

MAKES ABOUT ½ CUP

½ cup sour cream

1 to 2 canned chipotle chiles, finely minced (since they're hot, maybe start with 1, then you can add more)

Juice and zest of 1 lime—no zester, no big deal, just leave it out

1 tablespoon chopped fresh cilantro

1. Mix everything together in a small bowl.

2. If you have a spare squeeze bottle, I'd put it in there—it just makes it easier to use.

GARLIC AIOLI

In our restaurants, we put this s*** on everything.

MAKES ABOUT ½ CUP

½ cup mayonnaise

1 tablespoon minced garlic

1 tablespoon oil

1 tablespoon finely chopped curly parsley

1½ teaspoons fresh lemon juice

1 good pinch of kosher salt

1. Combine all the ingredients in a small bowl and mix really well.

2. Refrigerate until ready to use.

GUACAMOLE

All guac is not created equal. And if you think that's my way of saying this simple version is better than others . . . you'd be right.

MAKES ABOUT 2 CUPS

2 ripe avocados (ask a produce person if you don't know, but it should yield to gentle pressure because you can't do anything with an unripe one), peeled and pitted

½ medium tomato, seeded and diced small

¼ medium white onion, diced

Juice of 1 lime

1–2 canned chipotle chiles, finely minced

2 tablespoons chopped fresh cilantro

Pinch of kosher salt and freshly ground pepper

1. Place the avocado meat (what else would you call it . . . because flesh is worse, no?) in a bowl. Use a fork to mash it up a bit—I say a bit because we're trying to keep it chunky.

2. Add everything else and stir well to combine.

3. To store, transfer to an airtight container with a piece of plastic wrap literally lying on the surface of the guac before you add the lid—this will help keep it from turning brown.

PICO DE GALLO

I think the combo of jalapeño *and* serrano makes for some nice heat but not too much. But if you're not a fan, lose the serrano and double up the jalapeño.

MAKES ABOUT 2 CUPS

4 ripe Roma tomatoes, seeds removed and finely diced—you saw I wrote "ripe," yes?

½ cup loosely packed fresh cilantro, chopped

½ cup finely diced white onion

1 jalapeño pepper, seeded and diced small

1 serrano pepper, seeded and diced small

1 garlic clove, minced

Juice of 1 lime

½ teaspoon kosher salt

Put all the ingredients in a medium bowl and mix well to combine. Can definitely be made in advance—in fact, should.

INDEX